WHAT YOU ALWAYS WANTED TO KNOW ABOUT

CRAPS

BUT WERE AFRAID TO BET

D0801226

HUGH HERITAGE

A GUIDE TO DICE GAME PLAY

INSTITUTE OF SCIENTIFIC RESOURCES

P. O. Box 636

HAWTHORNE, CALIFORNIA 90251

Institute of Scientific Resources,
P. O. Box 636, Hawthorne, CA. 90251

An ISR Book   83-90201-1

ISBN   0-913651-01-X

First Printing, January 1985

Manufactured in the United States
of America

ACKNOWLEDGEMENTS

I am deeply grateful to the many persons who have been supportive of the development and production of this book. Among these are:

   Mary Yvonne -English, literary and word prossing consultant.

   Hal " The Greek " Michalis- who provided critical review and comments from a player's view of the game.

   A'lyce Louise-Library research.

INTRODUCTION

CRAPS or DICE is without a doubt the most exciting game in the casino. All players including the introverts become very lively when bets begin to pay off and a great deal of noise, shouting and casino excitement begins.

In the midst of all this activity an astute observer may notice that very _few_ players are completely knowledgeable of the game while a novice onlooker probably would believe that everyone at the table is an expert.

The lack of complete understanding provides the _greatest_ profits for the casino, not the built-in profit margins of the game, as most would like to believe.

This book is designed to tackle the Craps game head-on. It simplifies the complex game into easily understandable components. It is a complete study of the game in every detail and organized for easy reader reference.

This book removes the mystery and shows the game for what it is, "a business venture." It introduces the player to a common sense and technical approach of understanding, organizing and playing so that when runs occur the player can take full advantage of the business venture _profits_.

FORWARD

This book grew out of many, many years of research and crap table experience in casinos throughout the free world. Detailed studies and observations were conducted of the player information, too often misinformation, beliefs, playing patterns, attitudes, superstitions, desires, expectations, greed and etc.

Today's advanced technology provides the tools to do indepth analysis. Mathematical expressions for each area of the crap table were written in equation form and solved simultaneously in search for a flaw in this game that would put the player at a foolproof mathematical advantage.

There are none - the crap table is a sound game with some statistical percentages always in favor of the casino operators.

Then how can one ever win would be the natural question? Answer: by taking advantage of all the factors found in these studies in which the casino <u>cannot</u> <u>control</u>.

That's what this enclosed text is all about. Read it with an open mind. May the benefits that come with knowledge be yours.

CONTENTS

CONTENTS (Continued)

FIGURES

TABLES

THE BIG STORY

WHAT'S IT ALL ABOUT?

A capsule summary of the book and a guide to its usage.

DISCUSSION

"The craps game looks like so much fun, I wish I knew how to play," CRAPS, that is! If you've heard this once from the many spectators standing around watching a crap game in progress then you've heard it hundreds of times. That's just the spoken words from the spectators. Imagine how many participating players in the game are also thinking these same thoughts.

What makes the craps game the most exciting of all the casino games? It's the ACTION. There are so many different areas on the table on which to bet. One can make most of these bets at any time and several of them at the same time. What other game could even come close to providing this much action?

Why is everybody so reluctant to play this exciting game? Is it because it looks so complex? Just a glance at this complicated looking green felt is enough to discourage anyone. Once understood, however, it becomes a simple fun game.

Now for the first time, anyone who may be interested in playing the craps game, simply can.

This book will dissect the complicated looking game and present it in such a simplified manner that anyone will be able to understand it.

It will explore every conceivable facet of the crap game and provide an easy reference so that one can instantly put his fingers on any desired detail of the game. It is not necessary to wade through chapters of data searching for the answers. It will instruct you on all you'll ever want to know about this game. It's loaded with inside tips that only many years of studies and casino experience can produce. One only needs to read the parts which interest him.

With only a 30 minute scan of this book (perhaps during the ride from the airport to the casino), you will enter the world of the wild green felt, watch it become stripped to its bare essentials before your very eyes and then easily presented in a highly organized and simplified fashion.

This book contains the information for everyone interested in playing this exciting

game of chance. It is organized to make anyone
look like an expert after only a few minutes of
reading.

The enthusiastic investor in the game of
chance will want to keep this handbook of craps
either under his pillow or right next to the
best sold book in the world. This will allow
him, within an arm's reach, at all times of
need, when nothing else seems to work, to have
access to the important information in all
areas of life or death.

Most everyone has had the sad experience
of picking up a book and trying to quickly find
the data they want in it. Much wasted time is
spent flipping from contents to text generally
through the entire book while attempting to
find the particular reference and material that
one seeks. That's not the case with this
book. It is organized to allow the reader to
put his finger upon any desired part of the
data at any time he wishes.

Each area of instruction stands on its own
in that it contains all of the information
necessary for that area of play as well as the
references to other associated areas of the
book which may be helpful. If for some reason
you don't have the 30 minutes to read the book
before getting to the casino, then simply turn
to the Win-Loss Table XII. This table contains
in simplified form, all the data that you need
to begin play.

This book starts right out by showing the
player; HOW TO PLAY or SIMPLIFYING THAT WILD
GREEN FELT. The player is moved directly to
each area. It allows the player to get into
the game. Every area of the table that

you've ever dreamed of and some that you've never heard of is contained in these subchapters.

THE ODDS, ODDS, & ODDS explains all the mysteries for those players who now understand how to play the game and want to become at odds with a larger investment capability.

After learning all there is to the physical play on the dice table, the player is introduced to INSURANCE. This provides the know how necessary to protect the invested capital (bet).

When entering the arena of HOW TO WIN, we begin to see who wins, who loses and why.

We've all been introduced to rumored betting systems that can wipe the casino out. If you believe in them, don't read this chapter. BETTING SYSTEMS, HERE'S MORE provides a practical insight into using some progressive systems so that when the game is in your favor it will help multiply your riches.

AN EXPERT ON YOUR FIRST TRIP allows you to look and feel the role of an experienced craps gambler even with only the 30 minute trek through this handbook of craps.

Now that you know all about the game, what about DO's & DONT's? Maybe some of them apply to you or perhaps your own set of rules will be similar.

The CRAP TABLE OPERATION explains what's going on and who does what at the crap table.

Then, AH! YES, THE CASINO, here the player will be enlightened as to the smooth business of gambling entertainment.

A LITTLE HISTORY will help explain the well rooted gambling growth.

Then an explanation of THAT SILLY CUBE. One may become a little surprised to find how this simple looking cube plays it's character role across the stage of gambling.

WHO'S MANAGING THE MONEY? This is where the player learns how to take advantage of simplified money managing systems to help provide some free time for concentrating on the fun of gambling.

An introduction to the understanding of the winning opportunities in the game of chance through perception is within THE CRYSTAL BALL. Are you a perceptive gambler with insight yet to be discovered?

If you're a confirmed gambler you probably won't understand INVEST, DON'T GAMBLE. If you're interested in winning, then investing is what this game is all about.

Maybe you're one of the players who likes to put it all into the game. WINNER/LOSER, WHAT'S NEXT will help remind the player of the obvious goal; having some fun, winning and perhaps using some of the money for the finer pleasures of life.

WHAT ABOUT PROBABILITY? This section is designed for the player who may be interested in working out all the mathematics of the game.

WHO GAMBLES, WHY, WHO CARES will introduce you to the possible abnormality of those who say they have no desire to gamble. It provides some insight into man's heightened interest and excitement when testing that edge of the unknown. The urge to test lady luck seems to prevail in the species of man even in the days of your distant ancestory.

If you're interested in becoming a world

traveler and doing a little gambling along the way, GOING FOREIGN contains a brief discussion of world gambling.

If there are some terms within this book that don't mean anything to you, a quick look at the GLOSSARY will soon change all that and allow you to talk and sound like the rest of the players at the crap table.

The explanation of each area of the crap table play contains headings of HOW TO PLAY, EXAMPLE, DISCUSSION and TECHNICAL STUFF. How to play and example will provide one with the bare essentials for play. Discussion, contains more detailed information about the play area. Technical stuff explains the technical aspects for that area of play.

Now that you know what it's all about, waste no more time attempting to read the entire book. Simply look at the Table of Contents and find the subject matter that spins your motor up, read it, learn it, and get on with the exciting game of craps.

For those who want a quick guide to the bare essentials of this game, turn first to: HOW TO PLAY or SIMPLIFYING THAT WILD GREEN FELT, for the areas of gambling that tingle your excitement switch; then turn directly to AN EXPERT ON YOUR FIRST TRIP, then scan CRAP TABLE OPERATION, HOW TO WIN and you're ready to begin.

21

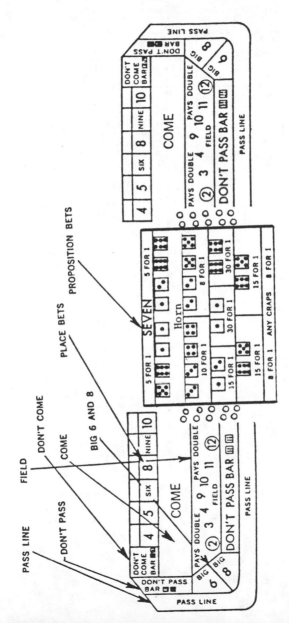

Figure 3
Dice Table Layout

WIN-LOSS   TABLE VII

Area		2	3	4	5	6	7	8	9	10	11	12
						Dice Numbers						
Pass	W			#	#	#	+	#	#	#	+	
	L	+	+				*					+
Don't Pass	W	+	+				*					
	L			#	#	#	+	#	#	#	+	
Come	W			#	#	#	x	#	#	#	x	
	L	x	x				*					x
Don't Come	W	x	x				*					
	L			#	#	#	x	#	#	#	x	
Place	W			#	#	#		#	#	#		
	L						*					
Field	W	o	o	o					o	o	o	o
	L				o	o	o	o				
Any	W	o	o									o
	L			o	o	o	o	o	o	o	o	
Hard-way 4	W			*								
	L			z			*					
Hard-way 6	W					*						
	L					z	*					
Hard-way 8	W							*				
	L						*	z				
Hard-Way 10	W									*		
	L						*			z		
Seven	W						o					
	L	o	o	o	o	o		o	o	o	o	o
Eleven	W										o	
	L	o	o	o	o	o	o	o	o	o		o
Two	W	o										
	L		o	o	o	o	o	o	o	o	o	o
Three	W		o									
	L	o		o	o	o	o	o	o	o	o	o
Twelve	W											o
	L	o	o	o	o	o	o	o	o	o	o	

W= Win   *= identifier
L= Loss   #= Point
o= 1 roll   += Come out roll
z= Easy way   x= First roll

HOW TO PLAY or

SIMPLIFYING THAT WILD GREEN FELT

WHAT'S IT ALL ABOUT?

Turning this complicated looking game into child's play.

SO WHAT ARE THE PERCENTAGES?

Shown on each play.

FIGURES AND TABLES

Figures 3 thru 11, Tables I thru VI

DISCUSSION

As one approaches the dice table, he may think that it looks very complicated with all the different numbers and arrangements of numbers spread out all over the green felt on this massive, large table. Many players in the casinos stay completely away from the craps game. They believe it to be far too complex to understand and play. The bulk of the gamblers who do surround the tables understand very little of what's going on. Most of their playing ideas have come from either copying other players or from some friend's stories.

The casino owners appreciate the contributions of the many uninformed players and certainly do not attempt to run a school on dice or the rules of the game. They do pass out brief one and two sheet instruction guides on the dice game. This shows a picture of the game and tells, in a one line description: How to play the Pass Line, Don't Pass, etc.

The crap table, once disassembled into its component parts becomes easily understood. The player will wonder why he has avoided this game for so long. After reading this chapter, one may be surprised as he watches the conversion of this initially complicated view become mere child's play.

The following text will take each part of the dice table and describe it with simplistic clarity so that anyone can easily understand how to play this complicated looking green felt.

It is the author's belief that the craps game is the fairest of the casino games. There are few methods that the casino could use to cheat the player even if they desired to do so. Crap games that the author has personally viewed around the world, over the years have shown that the casinos are interested in operating a completely fair, impartial and direct game.

The local libraries have little information available on the dice game. What is available is too general to give the player the details required to completely understand the game and to make bets intelligently. The bookshelves are full of gambling books but none explore the craps game to any real degree.

The casino advantages and profits are calculated based upon the laws of probability with a random distribution of the dice numbers over many rolls of play. It is, therefore, to the advantage of the casino to purchase the most perfect, best balanced dice cubes that are commercially available.

Viewing Figure 3, one can see that the dice table has the same markings on each side. The proposition bet area is located in the center. There is room for six to ten players to stand on each end of the table.

There are many different ways to play the crap game. They are completely explained in the text that follows. In addition, the house will usually entertain any reasonable bet which a player would like to make, if he simply asks the dealers to make that bet. Also the table limits will generally be lifted or raised for any player by just asking the house to extend these. The areas that will be discussed here are:

Pass Line	Proposition Bets	
Don't Pass	Seven	Eleven
Field	Horn	Hopping
Come	Hardways	Lays
Don't Come	C & E	
Big 6 & 8	Any Craps	
Place Bets	2, 3 & 12	

It is not necessary to shoot the dice in order to play the craps game. Some gamblers never shoot the dice, others always do and there are some gamblers who sometimes shoot them and sometimes do not.

There are some disadvantages to shooting the dice. The shooter must put a bet on the Pass Line or Don't Pass to shoot. He may have intended to bet some other area of the table and does not wish to be penalized by this bet.

Some gamblers are consistently very good at handling the dice. It appears when they shoot there is a fairly good chance of them having a good roll of the dice from the Pass Line or place bet position. In cases of this nature, the gambler has an advantage in betting on himself during the time that he is shooting the dice. There is no mathematical basis for this phenomenon.

Pass Line

WHAT'S IT ALL ABOUT?

A complete description of how to play the craps table area called, "Pass Line."

SO WHAT ARE THE PERCENTAGES?

On the come out roll, 22% to win; 11% to lose and 67% to get a point. On any roll after the come out roll, 8 to 14% to win and 17% to lose.

FIGURES AND TABLES

Figures 3 & 4, Tables I & II

HOW TO PLAY

The Pass Line is the most popular of all the crap table bets. It is also the easiest bet to make. You can put your bet on the Pass Line at any time. The Pass Line bet is locked into the game until the shooter completes his roll and then one either wins or loses. Once

28

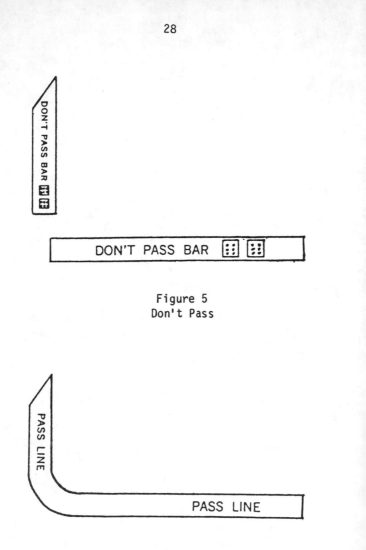

Figure 5
Don't Pass

Figure 4
Pass Line

the bet is made it cannot be picked up or
called off. There is really no effort to it.
Perhaps this is one reason that the Pass Line
is so popular. If you are the shooter you must
bet the Pass Line or Don't Pass in order to
have your turn at shooting the dice. All
players at the table may play the Pass Line at
any time.

Figures 3 and 4 show the layout of the
Pass Line on the crap table. The Pass Line
extends the entire length of each playing side
of the table. Normally, one would make the bet
on the Pass Line just before the shooter throws
his first come out roll of the dice. You may,
however, walk up to a table already in play and
bet the Pass Line if you wish.

If the shooter's come out roll is a 7 or
11, the player wins immediately. He loses if
the crap numbers 2, 3 or 12 are rolled. Any
other number that may appear on this come out
roll becomes the point number. These numbers
would be 4, 5, 6, 8, 9 or 10. Once the point
number is obtained the shooter must roll that
point number again before a 7 appears for the
player to win. The player will, of course,
lose on any 7 which appears after the point
number is obtained.

The player may choose to take the odds on
the bet once the point number is obtained. To
get a full explanation of odds betting, refer
to that chapter in the text and Table II.

EXAMPLE

Let's look at what this Pass Line bet is

all about. The player actually places the bet chips himself. These are put inside the bordered area designated as Pass Line.

A shooter picks up two dice and is ready to throw his come out roll. The dice are thrown to the opposite end of the table from the shooter. The sum of the combination of dots that appear when the dice come to rest is the dice number.

Let's suppose it is an 11. Since 11 is an instantaneous winner, the player would be paid an amount equal to his bet. This is done by the dealer putting a stack of chips next to the bet originally placed on the Pass Line. The player may remove some or all of the chips at this time.

On the next throw of the dice, the shooter throws a 3 craps. The Pass Line players lose. The dealer immediately picks up all the bets on the Pass Line.

The same shooter is ready for a new come out roll and all Pass Line players again make bets. Let's suppose the next come out roll of the dice is a 6. The 6 now becomes the point number. The dealer takes the marker from the end of the table and puts it in the box labelled 6. The shooter must throw the point 6 again before a 7 appears for the player to win.

Let's suppose there are several rolls of the dice in which all types of numbers including craps 2, 3, 12 and 11 appear (but no 7), and eventually a 6 appears. The Pass Line player would win and the dealer would pay them off.

If a 7 should appear before the point number is made, the Pass Line player loses and the shooter loses his turn with the dice. The dice would then be given to the next player/shooter located in a clockwise position around the table.

DISCUSSION

For a shooter to retain the dice, he must continue to pass or throw series of groups of numbers without the 7 appearing after a point is established. The shooter may throw on his come out roll, any one of the crap numbers. This will cost him bet chips on the Pass Line but he does not lose his shooting position. He may on his come out roll throw many 7's and 11's. In this case, he gets paid and retains his shooting position. He may establish a point many times. If he remakes that point, he keeps the shooting position. It is only after he establishes a point and then throws a 7 before he makes the point that he loses his position to shoot.

If a player joins a game in progress and puts a bet on the Pass Line, the casino dealer will usually remind him that he is betting on an already established point number. This is done to alert the player that he has entered a game in which he has taken a numerically disadvantaged bet position. The way to determine whether the game is in progress or not is to look for the marker. The table dealer keeps the marker at the edge of the table in the area called, "Don't Come," with the marker displaying "OFF." The marker displays "OFF" on one side and "ON" on the other side. Until the shooter makes a point number the marker is left in the "OFF" position. Once the point number is obtained the marker is flipped to the "ON" side and moved to the point number in the appropriate box.

Quite often, being around the dice table with players that are not paying too much attention or are not very knowledgeable of the game; they will see the dealer sweeping up all the Pass Line bets and they will make comments like: "What was the number?" or "What happened?" When one sees the sweep occur, it is obvious that a 7 has been thrown before the Pass Line point was made. It is sometimes difficult with all of the loud noises and from one's position at the crap table to see the number rolled or hear the stickman call out that number.

The Pass Line is an even bet, the player wins and gets paid the amount equal to the amount that he has bet regardless of the point number. If he loses, the funds are picked up by the casino dealer. The player may also improve his profits by betting the odds. The odds bets are paid as a true return on the point number probability. The odds bet is made by putting the appropriate amount of chips just outside of the bordered area marked Pass Line, on the players side, directly behind the original Pass Line bet. See the chapter, THE ODDS, ODDS & ODDS, to determine the proper quantities to bet.

TECHNICAL STUFF

The Pass Line bettor has the upper hand in the game on the come out roll of the dice. After that it changes. On the come out roll of the dice the player wins if a 7 or 11 are rolled. There are six ways in thirty-six to make a dice number 7; two ways in thirty-six to make the 11. This gives the Pass Line player eight ways in thirty-six to win on the come out roll or about 22%.

He loses if craps 2, 3 or 12 appear. There is one way in thirty-six to make a dice number 2; two ways in thirty-six to make a 3 and one way in thirty-six to make a 12. This gives a total of four ways in thirty-six or about 11% to lose. This is about a 2 to 1 advantage on the come out roll for a win versus a loss.

If the come out roll of the dice is not a 7, 11, 2, 3 or 12 then it is one of the point numbers, 4, 5, 6, 8, 9 or 10. On the come out roll a player has a chance of about 67% in obtaining a point number. When the point number is obtained the player has an 8% to 14% chance to win and a 17% chance to lose. His chances to win depend upon which Pass Line point number is obtained.

Table I shows the ways in which the dice numbers can be made. There are three ways in thirty-six to make a point number 4 or 10; four ways in thirty-six to make a point number 5 and 9; and five ways in thirty-six to make a point number 6 or 8. This provides a spread of approximately 8% to 14% for a win on numbers 4 and 6, respectively. There are six ways in thirty-six for a 7 to appear which totals about 17% to lose.

Taking the odds on the Pass Line bet will increase the amount that the player can win should this Pass Line point reappear. Some casinos allow double odds and even triple or more odds. One should make this inquiry before playing. On a hot game, this is a tremendous advantage to the player. The chances of win or loss, however, are not altered by taking the odds, just the amount of money that one could win should the point numbers begin to appear. The odds betting allows a higher return on the invested capital only.

Dice No's	Odds	Ways to make Dice Numbers					
		1	2	3	4	5	6
2	1/36	1 & 1					
3	2/36	1 & 2	2 & 1				
4	3/36	3 & 1	1 & 3	2 & 2			
5	4/36	3 & 2	2 & 3	4 & 1	1 & 4		
6	5/36	3 & 3	4 & 2	2 & 4	5 & 1	1 & 5	
7	6/36	4 & 3	3 & 4	5 & 2	2 & 5	6 & 1	1 & 6
8	5/36	4 & 4	5 & 3	3 & 5	6 & 2	2 & 6	
9	4/36	5 & 4	4 & 5	6 & 3	3 & 6		
10	3/36	6 & 4	4 & 6	5 & 5			
11	2/36	5 & 6	6 & 5				
12	1/36	6 & 6					

Table I
Dice Numbers

Don't Pass

WHAT'S IT ALL ABOUT?

A description on how to play the dice table area called, "Don't Pass."

SO WHAT ARE THE PERCENTAGES?

On the come out roll, 8% to win, 22% to lose and a 70% chance of getting a Don't Pass point. On any roll after the come out roll, 17% to win and 8% to 14% to lose.

FIGURES & TABLES

Figures 3 & 5, Table I

HOW TO PLAY

The Don't Pass is played just the opposite of the Pass Line. One exception is when a craps 12 occurs on the come out roll, it is a standoff. The house does not pay the Don't Pass for the bet nor do they take it.

Figures 3 and 5 show this layout area of

the crap table. The Don't Pass is just behind the Pass Line. It extends, generally, around the table so that there's easy access for players.

The Don't Pass bet must be made before the shooter throws his pass line come out roll of the dice. If, on the come out roll a 2 or 3 craps appear, the Don't Pass player wins instantly. If a 7 or 11 appear, he loses. If a craps 12 appears, it is a standoff.

Any other number that could appear being 4, 5, 6, 8, 9 or 10 would become the Don't Pass point. The shooter must not throw this number before a 7, for the player to win.

When a 7 is thrown after the Don't Pass point is established the player wins.

Once the Don't Pass point has been established the player may place odds on the bet. This is explained fully in the chapter on Odds betting.

EXAMPLE

A player is selecting the dice for shooting. The Don't Pass player has his bet in the Don't Pass area of the table.

Let's suppose the shooter throws the dice and a 2 craps appears. Since that is an instantaneous winner, the Don't Pass player wins. He would be paid an amount equal to his bet.

This is done by the dealer putting a stack of chips next to the bet originally put on the Don't Pass. The player may remove some or all of the chips at this time or continue to bet and play the Don't Pass area.

Let's suppose on the next roll the shooter throws a 7. The Don't Pass player would lose. His money would be removed from the bet area by the casino dealer.

The Don't Pass player again makes a bet putting it in the proper area. The shooter throws a number 10. The 10 now becomes the Don't Pass player's point.

The shooter continues throwing various numbers and finally throws a 7. The Don't Pass player wins. If the 10 was thrown before a 7 appeared the Don't Pass player would lose.

DISCUSSION

The player should not confuse the Don't Pass bet with the Don't Come bet. These bet areas are right next to each other but they are completely different games.

A shooter or any player may bet the Don't Pass area of the table. It would be nice if the Don't Pass player could make the bet after the pass line point is established because he would have the mathematical odds always in his favor.

This, of course, cannot be done although some players will intentionally try to put a bet on the Don't Pass after the point is established. They may attempt this when the casino dealer is busy in another area of the table. Most table dealers are familiar with this intentional and accidental type of bet. They are quite aware of all bets that are being played on their area of the table.

One of the good features about the Don't Pass bet is that it is removable by the player. If one were to change his mind after the point is established about wanting to continue the Don't Pass bet, he can simply pick it up.

The Don't Pass player may place the odds once the point has been established. This is done by putting the proper quantity of chips alongside and capping his initial bet.

This is different than the pass line player odds action. In this case, when the odds are taken, he puts the odds chips outside of the pass line area on the player's side of the table. To understand the odds betting, refer to that chapter.

TECHNICAL STUFF

The Don't Pass player has a real disadvantage on the Pass Line come out roll. The disadvantage is about two to one. After the point is established the game changes favorably to his side.

The player wins if a 2, 3 craps are thrown on the come out roll. Viewing Table I, one can see that there is one way in thirty-six to make the dice number 2 and two ways in thirty-six to make the 3. This is a total of three ways in thirty-six or about an 8% chance to win.

He loses if a 7 or 11 is rolled. There are six ways in thirty-six to make a 7 and two ways in thirty-six to make an 11. This totals eight ways in thirty-six or a 22% chance to lose on the come out roll.

Once the Pass Line point has been established, the Don't Pass player would win if a 7 appears on any roll before the point is made. There are six ways in thirty-six to make a dice number 7. This is about a 17% chance to win.

He would lose if the Pass Line point number appears. The point numbers would be 4, 5, 6, 8, 9 or 10. Depending on the point obtained, the Don't Pass player has an 8% to 14% chance of losing. There are three ways in thirty-six to make a dice number 4 or 10. This equates to about 8%. There are five ways in thirty-six to make a dice number 6 or 8. Which equals about 14%. This provides the spread of 8% to 14% to lose.

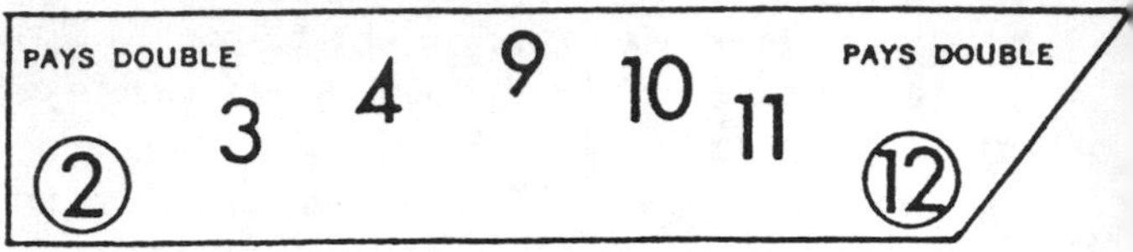
PAYS DOUBLE
3
4
9
10
11
PAYS DOUBLE
2
12

Figure 6
Field

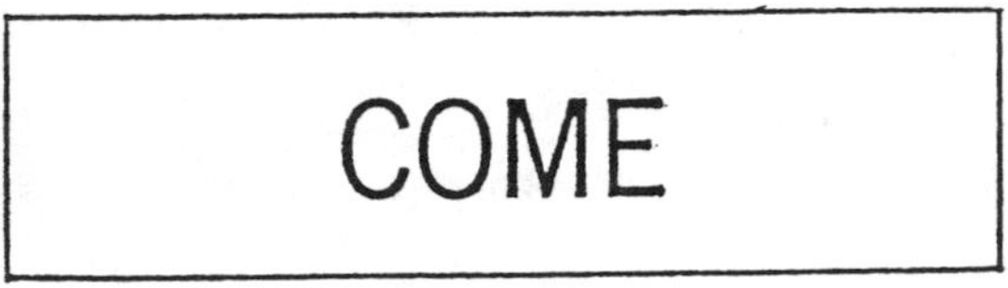
COME

Figure 7
Come

DON'T
COME
BAR

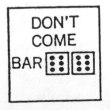

Figure 8
Don't Come

Field

WHAT'S IT ALL ABOUT?

This is a complete description of the dice table "Field" betting area along with all the information needed to understand this portion of the crap game.

SO WHAT ARE THE PERCENTAGES?

44% to win, 56% to lose.

FIGURES & TABLES

Figures 3 & 6, Table I

HOW TO PLAY

The Field is an easy area of the table to bet. It is located right in the center of each side of the dice table. It has easy access for all players. The Field is a one roll bet. The chips are simply placed or bet in the Field before the shooter rolls the dice. The player either wins or loses after each roll of the dice. Looking at Figures 3 and 6 of the "Field" area, one may find it very interesting to see that the player wins on so many dice numbers. The numbers 2, 3, 4, 9, 10, 11 and 12 are shown in this area and if any one of these numbers appear on the dice, the player wins. For dice numbers 2 and 12, the player wins double and in some casinos, triple. When looking at this group of numbers the only ones missing are 5, 6, 7 and 8. Of course the player loses should these crap cube numbers appear. Let's look at an example of play.

EXAMPLE

A shooter has the dice and is prepared to throw them. A player bets the Field area placing the money inside the border designated "Field." The shooter throws the dice and a 9 appears. The player will be paid by the casino. This is done by placing a quantity of chips equal to his bet, beside his bet. The player may at that time withdraw all of the funds, leave some or all for the next roll. On the next roll a 12 appears. The 12 on this table pays double. The casino dealer places funds equal to double that of the player's bet, next to his bet chips. Again, this may be either withdrawn in part, whole or left as the next bet. On the next roll the shooter throws a 6. Since a 6 does not appear in the Field numbers, the player loses the money. The house dealer simply picks it up.

DISCUSSION

The unsuspecting player may think that his chances of winning in the "Field" are very good. Of course, the four numbers missing have the highest chance of appearing. The Field is a very popular bet area. This is probably not only due to its location in the center of the playing area but also because so many numbers are contained within the box. This leaves the player with the thought, that it may be easy to win in this area. There is no intention, in this chapter, to play down the Field as a bet area. At times, as any player spending much time around the crap table would observe, there are runs of Field numbers in which many passes occur before any number other than a Field number appears. During these runs a great deal of money can be made playing the Field. The Field is highly advertised or touted by the stickman. When he calls the point rolled he will usually call out, for example: "Four, pay the Field!" even though there are no bets in the Field at the time.

In the chapter, THAT SILLY CUBE, the discussions of the dice physics may be of interest to the player in this area since the physical properties of the cube have some slight advantage toward dice numbers 2 and 12. The player may read that section to further his understanding on the dice cube.

TECHNICAL STUFF

Let's consider the numbers that provide

wins and losses for the player in the Field area. The numbers that win for the player are: 2, 3, 4, 9 10, 11 and 12. Viewing Table I, one may see that there is one way out of thirty-six to make the dice number 2; two ways to make the dice number 3; three ways to make the dice number 4; four ways so make the dice number 9; three ways to make dice number 10; two ways to make dice number 11; and one way to make the dice number 12. This gives a total of sixteen ways in thirty-six for the player to win, which equates to something like about 44%.

On the losing side, the numbers on which the player loses are: 5, 6, 7 and 8. Similarly, there are four ways in thirty-six to make the dice number 5; five ways to make a 6; six ways to make a 7 and five ways to make an 8. Looking at these totals, one would come up with twenty ways in thirty-six or almost 56%. The chance of loss on any one roll of the dice is obviously larger than the opportunity to win.

The house policy of paying double or triple (as the table may be labelled) for dice numbers 2 and 12 doesn't change these odds of winning or losing at all. It does, however, increase the quantity in which the player may win should numbers 2 and 12 appear. The percentage of wins/losses remain the same.

Come

WHAT'S IT ALL ABOUT?

Complete instructions on how to play the area of the dice table called, "Come."

SO WHAT ARE THE PERCENTAGES?

On the come out roll, 22% to win, 11% to lose and 67% to get a come point. On any roll after the come out roll, 8% to 14% to win and 17% to lose.

FIGURES AND TABLES

Figures 3 & 7, Tables I & II

HOW TO PLAY

The Come is played exactly like the Pass Line except that the bet is placed within the bordered area called, "Come." The Come point becomes the very next roll after the bet is made. The Come bet may be made anytime after a shooter has obtained his point on the Pass Line.

The player has an instant win if the come out
roll dice number is 7 or 11 and he loses if the
crap numbers 2, 3 and 12 are rolled. Any other
number that may come up on this roll becomes
his come point number. These numbers would be:
4, 5, 6, 8, 9 or 10.

Once the come point number is obtained the
shooter must roll that number again before a 7
appears for the player to win. The player
will, of course, lose on any 7 which appears
after the come point is obtained. The player
may choose to take odds on the bet once the
come point is made. To get a full explanation
of odds betting, refer to the chapter, THE
ODDS, ODDS AND ODDS. The location of the come
bet area is illustrated in Figure 3, dice table
layout and Figure 7, the Come area.

NOTE: DO NOT PLAY THE COME BET AREA, READ THE
DISCUSSION AND THE "PLACE BET" CHAPTER FOR A
SMARTER WAY TO DO BUSINESS.

EXAMPLE

The shooter has the dice and has obtained
a Pass Line point number. Either the very next
roll or several rolls later a player decides to
make a Come bet. He places his bet in the area
called "Come." The shooter throws the dice and
the combination of dice numbers becomes the
player's point. Let's suppose the shooter
threw an 11. Since that's an instant winner
the player would be paid an amount equal to his
bet. This is done by the dealer putting chips
next to the bet originally placed in the Come

area.

On the next throw of the dice, the shooter rolls a 5. The player's Come point is now 5 and the dealer takes the chips from the Come area and moves it to the numbered region directly behind the Come area and puts it in the block designated as 5. At this time the player may take the odds on the bet. Let's suppose the shooter continues shooting and eventually throws a 5 again. The dealer removes the money from the 5 area. He places an equal amount to it plus whatever is due the odds arrangement, if the odds are bet, and returns it to the Come area where the player can retrieve his winnings. Of course, in the case where the shooter may throw a 7 before the Come point is made, the player would lose.

Suppose the shooter makes his Pass Line point before the come player's come point is made and that the come player has taken the odds. Let's further then suppose that the shooter throws a 7 on his first Pass Line come out roll. The Come player would lose his Come bet but the odds bet would be returned to the Come player.

DISCUSSION

The player should not be confused with the Come point number relative to the Pass Line number. The Come bettor is playing a completely separate game with each roll of the dice that he bets in the Come area. Any number of players may make Come bets at the same time including the shooter on all rolls except the shooter's Come out Pass Line roll of the dice.

The casino dealer, in order to maintain an orderly payoff and knowledge of which player makes what bet on the Come, will place the Come bet in a position within the number box which equates to the location at the table of the betting player. This makes it easy for him or any other dealer who may fill in for him during break times to payoff the bets properly.

Although the Come area of the table is probably the second most active area, with the Pass Line being the first, there is a better way to obtain this same coverage without the locked up risk of betting the Come. Few players have thought about this concept and most books that have been written on dice discuss the best method of winning as betting the Come and taking the odds. Instead, the place bet area may be utilized. It is far more effective to place bets. These bets pay odds without having to take the odds and the bets can be called off whenever the player wishes. Whereas, the Come area bets are locked in until the termination of the game.

Table II shows the proper odds relationship for any Come point number, such that the player may be able to take the proper odds, should he choose to do so.

TECHNICAL STUFF

Like the Pass Line player, the Come bettor has the upper hand in the game on the very first roll of the dice. After that, it changes. On the first roll of the dice or the come out roll for the new Come player, the player wins if a 7 or 11 are rolled. There are six ways in thirty-six to make a 7 and two ways in thirty-six to make the 11. This gives the Come player eight ways in thirty-six to win on the come out roll or about 22%. He loses if craps 2, 3 or 12 appears. There is one way in thirty-six to make the 2; two ways in thirty-six to make the 3; and one way in thirty-six to make the 12. This gives him a total of four ways in thirty-six or about 11% to lose. There is about a two to one advantage on the Come out roll for win versus loss.

If the first roll of the dice is not a 7, 11, 2, 3 or 12 then it is one of the point numbers 4, 5, 6, 8, 9 or 10. On the come out roll the player has a 67% chance of obtaining a point. When the Come point is obtained the player has from an 8% to 14% chance to win and a 17% chance to lose. His chances to win depend upon the Come point number obtained. Table I shows the ways in which the dice numbers can be made. There are three ways in thirty-six to make a point number of 4 or 10; five ways in thirty-six to make the point number 6 or 8. This provides a chance of approximately 8% to 14% for the win. Of course, a 7 makes one a loser. There are six ways in thirty-six for a 7 to appear which totals about 17% to lose.

Taking the odds on the come point numbers will increase the amount the player can win should his come points reappear. The chances of win or lose are not altered by taking the odds.

Don't Come

WHAT'S IT ALL ABOUT?

Instructions on how to play the dice table area called, "Don't Come."

SO WHAT ARE THE PERCENTAGES?

On the come out roll, 8% to win and 22% to lose. On any roll after the come out roll it is 17% to win and 8% to 14% to lose.

FIGURES AND TABLES

Figures 3 & 8, Tables I & III

HOW TO PLAY

The Don't Come is played exactly like the Don't Pass except that the bet is placed in the bordered area called, "Don't Come." The Don't Come point is the dice number that appears on the very next roll, after the bet is placed. The Don't Come bet may be made anytime after the shooter has obtained his point on the pass line.

The player has an instant win if the come out roll dice number is 2 or 3 craps. He loses if the come out roll number is 7 or 11. If the come out roll is a 12 craps, it is a bar or stand-off. The house neither takes the chips nor do they pay the bet. Any other number that may come up on this come out roll becomes the Don't Come point. These numbers would be 4, 5, 6, 8, 9 or 10.

Once the Don't Come point number is obtained the shooter must not throw that point number again for the player to win. The player wins any time a 7 appears. If the Don't Come point is thrown before a 7, the player loses.

EXAMPLE

The shooter has the dice and has obtained a pass line point. Either the very next roll or several rolls later a player decides to make a Don't Come bet. He places his bet in the area called, "Don't Come." The shooter throws the dice and the combination of dice numbers on that roll becomes a player's Don't Come point.

Let's suppose the shooter threw a 2 craps. Since that is an instant winner, the player would be paid an amount equal to his bet. This is done by the dealer putting a stack of chips next to the bet originally put in the Don't Come area. On the next throw of the dice the shooter throws a 4. The player's

Don't Come point is now 4. The dealer takes the chip from the Don't Come area and moves it behind the numbered region. He puts it directly behind the block designated as 4. At this time, the player may place the odds on the bet.

Let's suppose the shooter continues shooting and eventually throws the 4 again. The dealer would pick up the chips (including the odds bet, if made) since the Don't Come player has lost. Let's suppose for a moment that the shooter does not throw a 4 again, but throws a 7 instead. The dealer moves the chips from behind the 4 area. He places an equal amount to it plus whatever is due from odds arrangement, if the odds are bet, and returns it to the Don't Come area where the player can pick up his winnings.

DISCUSSION

The player should not be confused by the Don't Come point number relative to the Pass Line number. The Don't Come bettor is playing a completely separate game with each roll of the dice when he bets in the Don't Come area. Any number of players may make a Don't Come bet at the same time including the shooter. These bets may be made on all rolls except the shooter's come out Pass Line roll of the dice.

The casino dealer, in order to maintain an orderly payoff and knowledge of which player makes what bet on the Don't Come, will put the Don't Come bet in a position within the box behind the numbers. This position will indicate the location at the table of the betting player. This makes it easy for him, or any other dealer who may fill in for him, to pay off the bets properly.

The Don't Come bet can be called down or removed at any time. This is a very important rule to know. At times this can save the player a lot of investment money, especially when a shooter begins to go into a long number shooting run. Also the Don't Come player may be conservative and would not like to bet against numbers such as 6 or 8 should they appear as the Don't Come point. This is easily handled by the player by simply telling the dealer, "No bet." The dealer will leave the bet chip in the Don't Come block. The player will get an opportunity or risk to see what the next roll will bring.

The Don't Come player may choose to place the odds on the Don't Come point once it is established. To get a full explanation of odds betting, refer to that chapter. The location of the Don't Come bet area is illustrated in Figures 3 and 8.

Table III shows the proper odds relationship for any Don't Come bet number. The player may place the proper odds, should he choose to do so.

TECHNICAL STUFF

Like the Don't Pass Line player, the Don't Come bettor has a poor hand in the game on the very first roll of the dice. After that it changes and becomes a game in the favor of the

Don't Come player.

On the first roll of the dice the Don't Come player wins if a 2 or 3 craps are rolled. There is one way in thirty-six to make a 2; two ways in thirty-six to make a 3; which gives a total of three ways in thirty-six or about 8% to win.

The Don't Come player loses if 7 or 11 are rolled. There are six ways in thirty-six to make a 7; and two ways in thirty-six to make the 11. This gives the Don't Come player eight ways in thirty-six to lose on the come out roll, or about 22%.

One should notice that this is different from the odds on the Pass Line. The Pass Line player loses on 12 craps and the Don't Come player is barred from a win on 12 craps.

If the come out roll of the dice is not 7, 11, 2, 3 or 12 then it is one of the Don't Come point numbers which will be 4, 5, 6, 8, 9 or 10. On the come out roll the player has an opportunity of 67% to obtain a Don't Come point. Once the Don't Come point is obtained, the player has a 17% chance to win and an 8% to 14% chance of losing, depending upon which Don't Come number was rolled.

Table I shows the ways in which the dice numbers can be made. There are three ways in thirty-six to make a point number 4 or 10; and five ways in thirty-six to make the point number 6 or 8. This provides a chance of approximately 8% to 14% to lose. A 7 roll of the dice is a winner. There are six ways in thirty-six for a 7 to appear, which totals about 17% to win.

Placing the odds on the Don't Come point

numbers will increase the amount the player can win or lose. The chances of win or loss are not altered by the odds. The Don't Come player who does place the odds, however, invests substantially more risk capital into the game since he is placing the odds and not taking the odds as he would when playing the Pass Line or Come areas.

Big 6 & 8

WHAT'S IT ALL ABOUT?

Instructions on how to play the dice table area called, "Big 6 & 8."

SO WHAT ARE THE PERCENTAGES?

14% to win; 17% to lose for either 6 or 8.

FIGURES & TABLES

Figures 3 & 9; Table I

HOW TO PLAY

The Big 6 & 8 area of the crap table is located in the player's corner. It is easily accessible to the dice table players.

To bet the Big 6 & 8 put your bet chips directly in the bordered area on the Big 6 or 8. The casino pays off if the bet number is thrown in any dice number arrangement. This is not a one roll bet. The player only loses if a 7 comes up before the 6 or 8.

The bet may be made at any time. The chips may be picked up at any time should the player change his mind about betting that area.

If the player wins, the casino pays him an amount equal to his original bet on either number.

EXAMPLE

A player is standing at the table. He notices Big 6 & 8 and decides to bet one of them. He chooses Big 8 and places his chip on that area.

The shooter, on the very next roll of the dice, throws an 8. The table dealer pays the player an amount equal to that of his original bet.

This is done by the dealer putting the amount directly beside the player's bet. He may retrieve the money or leave it for a continued bet.

On the next roll of the dice the shooter throws a 7. The Big 8 bettor loses and the dealer collects all the chips.

DISCUSSION

The most outstanding thing to remember about Big 6 & 8 is that it should not be bet if funds larger than $6 are used as the single bet. The money can be put on the place bet area 6 & 8 and be paid the house odds.

The Big 6 & 8 are individual bets and must be bet separately. One bet does not cover both of them.

These numbers are made large and placed in a convenient spot on the table to get player attention. This area does get a lot of attention from the players standing around the table.

Anyone can bet Big 6 & 8 including the shooter. The bets are made by the player. They may be picked up by the player at any time. The player only loses on this area with a 7.

Any other dice number that would come up would have no significance upon the game. One will win if the 6 or 8 are made by any combination of the dice and lose if the 7 should appear.

Figures 3 and 9 show the general layout of the Big 6 & 8 on the table. Table I shows the arrangement of dice numbers to make a 6, 8 and 7.

TECHNICAL STUFF

The player wins if a 6 or an 8, whichever is bet, appears before a 7 is thrown. It can be seen from Table I that the 6 or 8 have an identical quantity of ways in which they can appear.

There are five ways in thirty-six to make the dice number 6, and five ways in thirty-six to make an 8.

There are six ways in thirty-six to make the dice number 7. This equates to a 14% chance to win on either Big 6 or Big 8 and a 17% chance to lose.

Figure 9
Big 6 & 8

4	5	six	8	nine	10

Figure 10
Place Bets

Place Bets

WHAT'S IT ALL ABOUT?

Complete instructions on playing the crap table area called, "Place Bets."

SO WHAT ARE THE PERCENTAGES?

On each roll of the dice:
For 6 or 8 - 14% to win & 17% to lose
For 5 or 9 - 11% to win & 17% to lose
For 4 or 10 - 8% to win & 17% to lose

FIGURES & TABLES

Figures 3 & 10, Tables I & IV.

HOW TO PLAY

As one can see by looking at Figures 3 and 10, the Place Bet area on the dice table is directly in front of the table dealer. There is one on each side of the table. This bet area is not within reach of the players and for a good reason. The table dealers place and manage all chips that are bet in this region of the table.

The Place Bet is usually made after a shooter makes a pass line point. To bet the Place Bet area the player need only throw the chips to the dealer and call out the number that he would like to bet. These numbers would be: 4, 5, 6, 8, 9 and 10.

The area must be bet in multiples of $5 for dice numbers 4, 5, 9 & 10: $6 for 6 & 8. Betting these amounts will provide the proper payoff. The Place Bet area can be played at any time by instructing the dealer as to your desires. It is automatically off for any come out roll on the Pass Line. It may be called "on," or "working" by the player by directing the dealer to do so.

This is not a one roll bet. The player will win if the selected place bet number appears in any arrangement. He loses if a 7 appears before that number comes up.

The Place Bet numbers may be called "on" for whatever time period the player would like to play them. The place bets can be called down or taken off as the player chooses. It's possible to bet one or two rolls and then remove the chips from that bet area. This is sometimes helpful in reducing or removing risk in a shaky game.

EXAMPLE

The shooter has thrown a Pass Line come out roll and has obtained a point; let's say 6. The player has decided that he would like to place bet the rest of the numbers.

He throws the appropriate quantity of chips to the table dealer and calls out place bet 4, 5, 8, 9 and 10. This would cost him a minimum of $5 for the dice number 4; $5 for the 5; $6 for the 8; $5 for the 9 and $5 for the 10 or $26 total.

The shooter throws the dice again and let's suppose a 4 appears. From the Table IV, the player can see that he will win 9 for 5 for the number 4 bet. The table dealer will pay him $9.

The bets will remain upon the numbers until called down or until a 7 appears. Let's suppose that several rolls go on with the player being paid for the wins as the place bet numbers appear.

Suddenly the player gets a little antsy about the game and calls all of his bets down. The dealer would then take the original bet chips off the numbers and return them to the player.

DISCUSSION

The Place Bet area of the table is not played by the general population of gamblers. From a common sense position, it should be the area of the table bet by the majority of the players.

If one were to Place Bet, for example, 4 or 10 the true odds on this point would be 2 to 1. If paid the true odds he should get paid $10 for the $5 bet. Instead the house pays $9 for the $5 bet on those numbers.

When bets are made on the table such as the Pass and Come the house simply pays even money no matter what the number. One can see the advantage of playing the Place Bet area and playing it properly.

An excellent feature about this Place Bet area is that these bets may be called on and off at any time. For areas of the table such as the Pass and Come, once a point is made, one is locked into the game until the shooter's roll is complete. The place bet advantage is that of withdrawing the bet should a player get an intuitive feeling that the shooter is about to complete his run of luck.

The player may call his bets off and then reinstate them without the table dealer actually taking the chips from the Place Bet area. He may also call the bet down. In such a case the dealer will return the original bet chips to the player.

Any player may play the Place Bet area including the shooter at any time. The rule of the table is that the Place Bets are off on a Pass Line come out roll of the dice. As soon as the Pass Line point is established then the Place Bets automatically work unless called off by the player. This continues until the point is made or a 7 appears.

In the chapter describing the Come area, it was noted that one should not play Come but should play the Place Bet area instead. The reader can see quite clearly by now that by place bets he can indeed have the house pay him odds of from 9 to 5, 7 to 5 or 7 to 6 and he can maintain complete control of the game. These bets can be called on and off at any time.

The Come bettor must put the chips in the Come area, wait for a come out roll to establish a point, then the money is moved to the numbered area. He gets paid only even money. His bet is locked up until the come roll is completed. If he takes the odds, he only gets paid the true odds payoff on the odds chips.

In betting the Place Bet area, all of this can be done with a much lower investment, lower risk and higher return for the same invested capital. Is that not what all investors are looking for?

If a player wins on the Place Bet area and wishes to double his bet then he uses the expression, "Press." This tells the dealer to double the original bet and return the remaining payoff funds to the player.

For example, if he had bet $5 on 10 and had won, the dealer would give him $9. He says, "Press," the dealer puts up another $5 making his bet now $10 and returns $4 to the player.

The Place Bet area of the dice table is definitely the best area for the investor/player. The sooner he obtains the working knowledge and finesse of operation in this area the quicker he will progress to the winning circle.

TECHNICAL STUFF

Viewing Table I, there are three ways in thirty-six to make a dice number 4 and also the same for the 10. This yields about 8% to win.

The only way to lose on these bets is for a 7 to appear. There are six ways in thirty-six to make a 7 which is about 17% to lose. Any other number which appears does not affect the Place Bet area at all.

For a 5, also a 9, there are four ways in thirty-six to make that number. This equates to approximately 11% to win for either number.

For the 6, also the 8, there are five ways in thirty-six for the 6 or 8 to appear. This is about a 14% chance to win.

The Table IV shows these place bet numbers in tabular form with the odds, and payoff for each of the numbers.

Place Bet Number	4	5	6	8	9	10
True Odds	3 in 36	4 in 36	5 in 36	5 in 36	4 in 36	3 in 36
House Odds	6 in 36	6 in 36	6 in 36	6 in 36	6 in 36	6 in 36
House Payoff	9 to 5	7 to 5	7 to 6	7 to 6	7 to 5	9 to 5

Table IV
Place Bets

Proposition Bets

The Proposition Bet area contains an opportunity for the player to have a lot of fun. It is located in the center of the craps table. All bets in the Proposition area are controlled by the stickman. The bets must be made by tossing the chips into the center of the table and calling out in a significantly loud enough voice for the stickman to hear you. Clearly state the bet you'd like to make.

Contained in this Proposition Bet area are "Seven," "Horn," "Hardways," "C & E," "Any Craps," "2," "3," "11," "12," "Hopping," and "Lay." Each one of these areas of play are described in detail in the following chapters with that heading. The Proposition Bet area can be seen by looking at the Figure 3 and Figure 11 table layout. Proposition Bets in general provide very high house profits, however, when groups of numbers begin to appear, the Proposition Bet area is another way for the player to take advantage of a good investment. The Proposition Bet area may be played at anytime by the shooter or any player.

The bet limits usually run from $1 minimum

to $500 maximum on any single bet. The player should watch out for his bet. The stickman has many people shouting at him and sometimes puts the chips in the wrong place. If this should happen, the player needs to get it straightened out before the dice are rolled.

The casino usually pays off the player, (when the Proposition Bets hit) while at the same time keeping the bet alive on the table. This adds greatly to the casino's percentage of profit. The player should be aware of this so he can call the bet chips down when it hits. That is, if he should choose that approach.

In the average game, the Proposition Bet area does not receive much attention from the players; nor is it bet much. It is believed that this is due to the fact that the majority of the players surrounding the table do not understand the betting rules in this area. Once someone at the table begins to play certain Proposition bet areas, it seems to avalanche to the rest of the players, especially if some player wins in this region.

Table VI conveniently shows the Proposition Bets, their true odds, and what the house pays.

Seven

WHAT'S IT ALL ABOUT?

Instructions on how to play the proposition bet area called, "Seven."

SO WHAT ARE THE PERCENTAGES?

17% to win and 83% to lose.

FIGURES & TABLES

Figures 3 & 11, Tables I & VI

HOW TO PLAY

The proposition bet area Seven is played by throwing the bet chip into the center of the table to the stickman and calling out, "Seven." He takes the bet chip and places it in the proposition area called Seven. This is a one roll bet. After the dice are thrown you either win or lose. There is no waiting for many rolls to see the outcome.

EXAMPLE

The shooter has the dice either on a come out roll or any roll and is ready to throw them. A player throws a chip to the center of the table and calls out, "Seven." The stickman places the chip in the area Seven.

The shooter throws the dice and a 7 appears. The stickman tells the table dealer on the betting player's side of the table that a specific player has won the bet. He also tells him the amount to pay the player.

The dealer then pays the player. The bet is left up automatically for another roll of the dice, unless the player calls it down.

DISCUSSION

The player must call down the bet if he wins and no longer wants the chips to ride for another roll. If not, when he wins, he's paid off (5 for 1) less the amount that's still on the bet. This is an amount equal the original bet. It remains there to win or lose on the very next roll of the dice.

Since this is a one roll bet the player wins or loses after each roll. The payoff for the proposition bet Seven is five for one or four to one. It's actually five times the bet unit that was made. If one made a bet of $1 and won, he would be paid $5. The casino keeps the $1 originally bet. If one accepts the normal payoff, he would be paid $4 and a $1 bet is kept up on the bet area. So the bet is really a four to one bet, expressed as five for one on the table. Bets may be made in multiples of $1 chips, up to the table limit, which is usually $500.

Figures 3 and 11 show the Proposition bet area. The Seven bet location is the upper row position. Table VI shows the odds and payoff for the Proposition bets.

TECHNICAL STUFF

Looking at Table I, there are six ways in thirty-six to make a dice number 7. There are thirty ways in thirty-six for any other number to appear on any one roll of the dice. This leaves the player with an opportunity of approximately 17% to win and 83% to lose on any roll of the dice.

Proposition Bet	True Odds	House Pays
Seven	6 to 1	5 for 1 or 4 to 1
Hardway 6	10 to 1	10 for 1 or 9 to 1
Hardway 8	10 to 1	10 for 1 or 9 to 1
Hardway 4	8 to 1	8 for 1 or 7 to 1
Hardway 10	8 to 1	8 for 1 or 7 to 1
Three	18 to 1	15 for 1 or 14 to 1
Two	36 to 1	30 for 1 or 29 to 1
Twelve	36 to 1	30 for 1 or 29 to 1
Eleven	18 to 1	15 for 1 or 14 to 1
Any Craps	9 to 1	8 for 1 or 7 to 1

Table VI
Proposition Bets

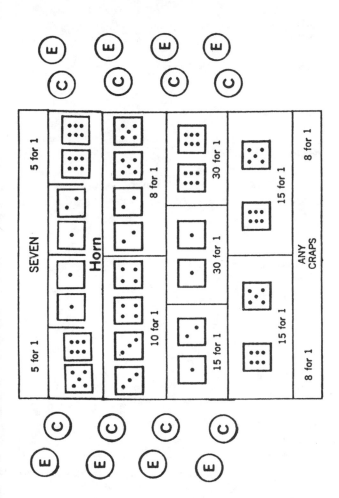

Figure 11
Proposition Bets

Horn

WHAT'S IT ALL ABOUT?

A complete description on how to play the proposition bet area of the crap table called, "Horn."

SO WHAT ARE THE PERCENTAGES?

17% to win and 83% to lose.

FIGURES & TABLES

Figures 3 & 11, Tables I & VI

HOW TO PLAY

The player tosses his bet chips into the center of the table and calls out, "Horn." The stickman takes the chips and places them within the block, "Horn."

Within this block the player will see that he has covered four bets: 2, 3, 11 and 12. This is a one roll bet. The player must bet at least $1 for each of these numbers or $4 minimum. He may bet more, or he may bet more on one or more of the numbers within the block.

When the dice are thrown the player either wins or loses. If he wins he is paid the appropriate amount of the payoff for that number which comes up on the dice.

EXAMPLE

Just before the shooter rolls, either the come out roll or any roll of the dice, the player tosses at least $4 to the stickman and calls for a Horn bet. The stickman places the chips in the bet area.

Let's suppose the shooter throws an 11. The house would pay the player fifteen for one for this dice number, but remember the casino always puts the bet back up unless it is called down. This means they would subtract $4 from the $15 and give the player $11 for his Horn bet.

Now suppose the dice are thrown again and a number 8 appears. The Horn bet player would lose. The stickman would clear the bets from the area.

DISCUSSION

Since the Horn bet contains the four numbers: 2, 3, 11 and 12, there are different payoffs depending on which of the numbers appear.

If a 2 or 12 would appear on the roll, the Horn bet payoff would be thirty for one or twenty-nine to one minus the four units that are automatically kept for the next bet, unless the player calls it down.

If a 3 or 11 is thrown the casino would pay fifteen for one or fourteen to one minus the four units for maintaining the bet on the next roll. The player may make unit bets on each of the Horn numbers in multiples from $1 to the house limit. For a $1 player the Horn bet would be $4, for a $5 player the Horn bet would be $20 and, etc.

It might be noted that any player can make the very same bet by individually betting 2, 3, 11 or 12 in the appropriate proposition bet area.

The Horn bet is primarily designed for people who just want to call, "Horn" and cover all these numbers. It also has a better built-in profit structure for the casino so they're happy to provide such a convenient bet location for the players. A player generally would not bet all these numbers if they were not so conveniently packaged.

Some players may throw a $5 chip to the stickman and bet "Horn Hi." This would mean $1 would be bet on each of the numbers 2, 3, 11 and 12 having the extra $1 bet or a $2 total bet. This bet can also be called "Horn Lo" or with any of the other numbers being 3 or 11.

TECHNICAL STUFF

Since this is a one roll bet, the opportunity for the player to win is based upon his obtaining one of the dice numbers: 2, 3, 11 or 12 on that one roll of the dice.

There are two ways in thirty-six to make a dice number 3 or 11. There is one way in thirty-six to make a 2 or 12. This gives the total for the Horn block of six ways in thirty-six or about 17% for a win.

There are thirty ways in thirty-six for one of the other numbers to appear or about 83% for a loss.

The decision to make a Horn bet is largely based upon the ease of betting all the craps numbers and 11 with just one bet. If one wanted to insure a Pass Line or Come bet on this come out roll it could be accomplished with less expense by betting Any Craps to protect against losses. This is discussed in detail in the chapter titled, INSURANCE.

Hardways

WHAT'S IT ALL ABOUT?

Complete information on how to play the proposition bet area called, "Hardways."

WHAT ARE THE PERCENTAGES?

On Hardways 4 & 10, 3% to win and 22% to lose.
On Hardways 6 & 8, 3% to win and 28% to lose.

FIGURES & TABLES

Figures 3 & 11, Tables I & VI

HOW TO PLAY

The proposition bet area called Hardways is played by throwing the bet chip to the center of the table and calling out, "Hardway," whichever number you would like to bet: "4, 6, 8 or 10."

The stickman puts your chip on the proper Hardway bet area. This is not a one roll bet. The player wins if the selected number comes up in pairs. He loses if a 7 is rolled or if the bet number appears in any other dice combination arrangement.

EXAMPLE

The player can make this bet at any time, just before the dice are thrown on any roll in the game. The player throws the chips to the stickman and bets $1 each on all of the Hardways: Hardway 4, Hardway 6, Hardway 8 and Hardway 10.

Let's suppose that the shooter throws the dice and a pair of 2's come up on the dice. The player would win on Hardway 4. The stickman would direct the dealer on the player's side of the table to pay the player eight for one which is actually seven to one. $7 is paid to the player and the bet is up for another roll.

Let's suppose that the player continues to throw the dice and a pair of 4's appear on the dice. The player wins on Hardway 8. Again the stickman instructs the dealer to pay the player ten for one or nine to one. The player is paid $9. $1 is left up as the bet.

The player may call this down should he choose to do so. He would then be paid $10. Let's suppose the shooter continues and throws a 7. The player loses and all of the chips are removed by the stickman.

DISCUSSION

The Hardway bet is an exciting area of the

table to play. Occasionally there are shooters
who will throw runs in which the Hardways
appear continuously. These bets pay handsomely
during such action. The player may call these
bets off at any time. The stickman will mark
the bet chip off without removing the bet for a
given number of passes. The player can call
them back on and they would be working for the
remaining series of rolls or the player may
decide at any time in the game to simply remove
his bet from that area. He could do that by
telling the stickman to take them down on the
Hardways. The stickman would remove the money
and instruct the dealer to return to the player
his original bet chips.

It may be noted from Table I that all of
the Hardways have the same opportunity to win.
There is only one way in thirty-six in which
they will appear. There are different ways for
the dice number to appear other than the
Hardway. That is why there is a difference in
payoff for the Hardways 6 and 8 versus the
Hardways 4 and 10.

The location of the Hardway bets may be
seen in the center of the proposition bet area
of the table by viewing Figures 3 & 11. Table
VI shows the proposition bets and payoff.

TECHNICAL STUFF

The Hardway player wins if the number
comes up in pairs. He loses if a 7 appears or
if the number appears in any other combination
other than the pairs bet.

Considering first the Hardway 4. There

is only one way in thirty-six to make the
Hardway 4. That is with a 2 on each dice.
This gives the player about a 3% chance to
win. There are two other ways to make a 4,
with a 3 on one dice and a 1 on the other.
There are six ways in thirty-six to make a 7.
This totals eight ways in thirty-six in which
the player can lose on Hardway 4 or about 22%
for a loss.

There is only one way in thirty-six to
make a Hardway 6. That is with a 3 appearing
on each dice. This yields about a 3%
opportunity to win on Hardway 6. There are
four other ways to make a 6. That is, with a 1
and a 5, 5 and a 1, 2 and a 4, 4 and a 2.
There are six ways in thirty-six to make a 7.
This gives ten ways in thirty-six for the
player to lose or about 28%.

There is one way in thirty-six to make the
Hardway 8. That is, with a 4 appearing on each
dice. This gives about a 3% chance of
winning. There are four other ways in
thirty-six to make the 8. This is done with a
5 and a 3, 3 and a 5, 6 and a 2, and a 2 and a
6. There are six ways in thirty-six for a 7 to
appear which gives a total of ten ways in
thirty-six or about 28% to lose. This is the
same as the Hardway 6.

There is one way in thirty-six to make a
Hardway 10 and that is with a 5 appearing on
each of the dice. This gives the player about
a 3% chance of win. There are two other ways
to make a 10: with a 6 and a 4, and a 4 and a
6. There are six ways in thirty-six to make
the 7. This gives a total of eight ways in
thirty-six or about 22% to lose.

C & E

WHAT'S IT ALL ABOUT?

Instructions and data on how to play the proposition bet area of the crap table called, "C" & "E."

SO WHAT ARE THE PERCENTAGES?

"C" is 11% to win and 89% to lose.
"E" is 6% to win and 94% to lose.

FIGURES AND TABLES

Figures 3 & 11, Tables I & VI

HOW TO PLAY

"C" & "E" are actually two separate bets. The "C" is the symbol for craps and is identically the same as betting, "Any Craps." The "E" is the symbol for Eleven and is identically the same as betting, "Eleven."

To play "C", throw the chip to the stickman in the center of the table and call out "C" or craps. The stickman will put the chip on the "C" in the proposition bet area. This is a one roll bet. If any one of the craps numbers 2, 3 or 12 appear the player wins. The player either wins or loses after each roll of the dice.

To play "E", throw the chip to the stickman and call out "E" or Eleven. The chip is moved to the "E" in the proposition bet area. It's a one roll bet like the "C" bet. If an 11 appears on that roll of the dice the player wins. Any other number that may appear is a player loss. If the player wins, the stickman directs the dealer to pay off the player.

EXAMPLE

Just before the shooter throws the dice, any roll of the dice, the player tosses the chips to the stickman and calls out, "C" & "E", or "C" or "E" or whatever combination he would like to bet. The stickman places the money on the bet and the dice are thrown.

Let's suppose the player has bet both "C" & "E". The dice are thrown; an 11 appears. The player would be paid on the 11 and would lose on the craps.

The stickman would direct the dealer to pay the player fifteen times the unit bet for the 11, but he would then deduct two units to put the bet back up again. Hence, the "C" & "E" bet would be paid off at thirteen times the unit bet. These bets, of course, can be called down by the player by simply telling the dealer that he wants his money down.

The shooter again throws the dice and this time a 3 craps appears. The player wins eight for one. The stickman directs the dealer to pay the player six times the unit bet having subtracted the two units and put the bet back up again. The bet may be called down as described in the above Eleven win example.

DISCUSSION

The "C" & "E" bet is exactly the same as betting the other area of the proposition bet called, "Any Craps" and "Eleven." These bets are individual bets. If one wishes to bet both, then he must call out both bets.

The categories "C" & "E" are placed there for the convenience of the player and dealer. With numerous players betting "Craps" and "Eleven," it is much easier for the stickman to put the chips on "C" & "E". It is also much easier to identify the payoff player with this arrangement since the bet chips can be placed in accordance with the player's table location.

Quite often players of the Pass Line like to bet "Any Craps" for insurance during come out rolls. At times they may also be very optimistic that an 11 will appear so they like to bet it. "C" & "E" are common bets among the Pass Line and Come players.

The convenience of setting "C" & "E" on the outside of the proposition block area helps facilitate the dealer's keeping track of the bet and table player. It also expands the room available for these bets.

The payoff for "C" is eight for one or seven to one. The bet is kept up (unless called down) automatically by the house.

The payoff for "E" is fifteen for one or fourteen to one. Again the bet is re-established for the player unless he specifically calls it down.

The location of the "C" & "E" may be seen by viewing Figures 3 and 11. The payoff structure is contained in Table VI.

TECHNICAL STUFF

Since the "C" & "E" are one roll bets, the player either wins or loses after each roll of the dice. Consider first the "C" or Craps, which are dice numbers 2, 3 or 12.

From Table I, one can see that there is one way in thirty-six to make a dice number 2; two ways in thirty-six to make a 3; one way in thirty-six to make a 12. This totals four ways in thirty-six or about 11% to win.

There are thirty-two ways in thirty-six for one of the remaining numbers to appear. This gives approximately 89% chance of loss on any one roll of the dice.

Consider now the "E" or Eleven. There are two ways in thirty-six to make a dice number 11. This totals about 6% to win.

There are thirty-four remaining ways in thirty-six for any other number to appear on that roll. This gives about a 94% chance of loss.

Any Craps

WHAT'S IT ALL ABOUT?

A complete description of how to play the proposition bet area of the dice table called, "Any Craps."

SO WHAT ARE THE PERCENTAGES?

11% to win and 89% to lose.

FIGURES AND TABLES

Figures 3 & 11, Tables I & VI

HOW TO PLAY

"Any Craps" is a one roll bet. It is played by tossing the chips to the center of the table and calling out, "Any Craps." The stickman places the bet in the proper area. The shooter throws the dice and if 2, 3 or 12 craps come up on that roll, then the player wins, if not the player loses.

The payoff on Any Craps is eight for one

or seven to one. If the player wins, the
casino automatically puts the bet back up.
This is subtracted from the winnings. He would
direct the table dealer to pay the player a
quantity seven times the original bet.

EXAMPLE

The shooter has the dice. Just before
he's ready to roll, the player bets Any Craps.
The shooter throws the dice and a 12 craps
appears.

The stickman directs the table dealer to
pay the player. An amount equal to the
original bet is left up as a bet for the next
roll of the dice. The player may call this bet
down.

The shooter throws the dice again and a 5
comes up. The player loses and the bet money
is picked up by the stickman.

DISCUSSION

The Any Craps bet is identical to betting
"C." The crap numbers can also be bet by
individually betting: 2, 3, 12. Or they can be
obtained by betting the Horn. The Horn, in
addition to the craps numbers also includes 11.

The good thing about betting Any Craps or
"C" is that one can make a bet in one area and
it covers all three of the craps numbers. Any
one of the numbers 2, 3 or 12 that would appear
would be a payoff for the player; whereas, the
others must be played with multiple bets.

The Any Craps area of the dice table can be seen in Figures 3 and 11. Table VI shows the odds and casino payoff. The Any Craps area of the table is usually bet as insurance to protect against loss on Pass Line or Come bets. See the chapter on INSURANCE to find proper use of Any Craps for this protection.

TECHNICAL STUFF

This is a one roll bet. The player wins on any one of the craps numbers that appear. These numbers are: 2, 3 or 12.

Viewing Table I, one can see that there is one way in thirty-six to make a dice number 2; two ways in thirty-six to make a 3; and one way in thirty-six to make a 12. This totals four ways in thirty-six or about an 11% chance to win.

Any of the other numbers that could appear on the dice during that one roll would equal thirty-two ways in thirty-six. This is about an 89% chance of losing on any one roll.

2, 3 & 12

WHAT'S IT ALL ABOUT?

Instructions on how to play the proposition bet area of the crap table called, "2," "3," & "12."

SO WHAT ARE THE PERCENTAGES?

For a 2, 3% to win, 97% to lose.
For a 3, 6% to win and 94% to lose.
For a 12, 3% to win and 97% to lose.

FIGURES AND TABLES

Figures 3 & 11, Tables I & VI

HOW TO PLAY

The 2, 3 and 12 are individual areas of the proposition bet and they must be bet that way. This is done by throwing the bet chip to the stickman and calling out, "2," "3," and "12" or whichever one of them you want bet.

This is a one roll bet. The player either

wins or loses after each roll of the dice. The stickman directs the dealer to make the payoff if the player wins or he gathers up the chips if the player loses.

Figures 3 and 11 show the table location of these proposition bets.

EXAMPLE

Just before the shooter throws any roll of the dice, a player tosses three chips to the stickman and calls for a bet on 2, 3 and 12. The stickman places the money in the appropriate blocks.

The shooter throws the dice and a 12 appears. The stickman instructs the dealer to pay the player, thirty for one or twenty-nine to one. The player would normally be paid twenty-nine times the unit bet by the dealer with a one unit bet left up for another 12 bet.

However, since this player has bet all three of these numbers, the dealer would hold out three times the unit bet and pay the player twenty-seven times the unit bet. All of the original bets would then be left up automatically for the next roll. To stop this, the player would have to call this bet off and down.

The next roll that is thrown is a 3. The stickman instructs the dealer to again pay the player and he is paid fifteen for one or fourteen to one. The dealer would give the player twelve times the unit bet. Three units would remain as the bet on the next roll of the dice.

On the next roll of the dice an 8 appears. The player loses all of his bets. These are picked up by the stickman.

DISCUSSION

Betting the 2, 3 or 12 has a higher individual payoff since the player is betting each specific number. All these crap numbers can be bet as one single unit by betting Any Craps or "C" in the proposition bet area.

When one bets 2, 3 or 12 they are betting those numbers individually. One may choose to bet only one of these numbers, two of them or all of them.

By viewing Table VI, one will see that the payoff for a 2 or 12 is thirty for one or twenty-nine to one. The payoff for 3 is fifteen for one or fourteen to one.

If the player chooses not to continue the play after it hits, he may call the bet down. In this case he would be paid the full fifteen times the unit bet for a three or thirty times the unit bet for a 2 or 12. He must act to do that or the bet will remain up for the next roll. The payoff would then be less the unit bet chip which will be removed and returned to the original bet area, instead of to the player.

In the chapter, BETTING SYSTEMS, HERE'S MORE, the X tables contain progressive betting systems for those especially fond of wagering these numbers.

These numbers do appear more frequently than the normal expected distribution with some dice because of the way in which the dice cubes are manufactured. One may also wish to review the chapter, THAT SILLY CUBE. It may generate more interest in betting these numbers.

TECHNICAL STUFF

This is a one roll bet. The player either wins or loses with each roll of the dice. When betting a 2 or 12, there is one way in thirty-six for this number to appear. This totals about a 3% chance to win.

There are thirty-five ways in thirty-six for any other number to appear. This gives about a 97% chance to lose on any roll of the dice.

When betting the 3, there are two ways in thirty-six to make the 3. This equals about 6% to win. There are thirty-four ways in thirty-six for any other number to come up on that roll. This totals about 94% to lose.

Tables I and VI show the dice number arrangement along with the true odds and casino payoff.

Eleven

WHAT'S IT ALL ABOUT?

Complete data on how to play the proposition bet area called, "Eleven."

WHAT ARE THE PERCENTAGES?

6% to win and 94% to lose.

FIGURES AND TABLES

Figures 3 & 11, Tables I & VI

HOW TO PLAY

The proposition bet area, "Eleven," is a one roll bet. It is located in the center of the table and managed by the stickman. The player throws the chip to the center of the table and calls out, "Eleven." The stickman places the chips on the appropriate bet area.

The player either wins or loses after each roll of the dice. If a dice number 11 appears, the player wins. For any other number that may come up, the player loses.

EXAMPLE

The shooter has the dice and is ready to roll. The player throws the chips to the center of the table and calls out, "Eleven." The shooter throws the dice and an 11 appears.

The stickman directs the table dealer to pay the player fifteen for one or fourteen to one. Since this bet is kept up unless called down by the player, the player is paid fourteen times the original bet. One bet unit is left up for the next roll of the dice.

On the next roll a 7 appears. The player loses and the chips are picked up by the stickman.

DISCUSSION

Betting the Eleven is also the same as betting "E" in the proposition bet area. The Eleven is sometimes bet by the Don't Come and Don't Pass players as insurance against loss on a come out roll.

It is also popular for some players who like to see an 11 appear on the dice. Bets may be made in multiples; $1 to the table limit, which is usually $500.

The Eleven area of the proposition bet may be seen by viewing Figures 3 and 11.

TECHNICAL STUFF

This is a one roll bet. The player wins or loses on any roll of the dice. From Table I, one can see that there are two ways in thirty-six to make the dice number 11. This represents about a 6% chance to win.

The opportunity for any other number on the dice to appear on that roll is thirty-four ways in thirty-six or about 94% to lose.

Tables I and VI show the ways that the dice numbers may appear and the proposition payoff for this area.

Hopping

WHAT'S IT ALL ABOUT?

A complete description of how to play the proposition bet called, "Hopping."

SO WHAT ARE THE PERCENTAGES?

6% to win and 94% to lose.

FIGURES AND TABLES

None

HOW TO PLAY

The proposition bet, "Hopping," is rarely played except by the old hands that are very knowledgeable of the game. Looking at the Figure 3 dice table, one will see no label for the bet, "Hopping." Hopping is a bet allowed by the casino for betting the numbers: 4, 5, 6, 7, 8, 9 or 10 in any arrangement in which one would like to call. This is a one roll bet. The bet chip is tossed to the stickman in the middle of the table. Let's look at an example of this seemingly complicated play.

EXAMPLE

A player may have an intuitive feeling that a number such as 4 and 1 will appear on the dice making a total dice number of 5. The player would toss the chip into the center of the table to the stickman and say, "4-1, Hopping." He could acquire the same 5 point via "3-2, Hopping."

At any rate, he calls, "4-1 Hopping" and the shooter rolls the dice. A 4-1 appears on that roll of the dice and the stickman directs the table dealer to pay the proper bet chips to the player. If any other combination of numbers appear on that roll, the player would lose.

DISCUSSION

A merchant has a store. His clientelle wished to procure something that he doesn't have in stock. He generally is very interested in finding out their need so he can provide it to the customer. There is a profit involved in his providing such services. The store and the overhead are already paid.

The casinos also attempt to provide good service to keep their customers. They would like to allow any reasonable wagering that a player would like to make. Hopping is just such a wager.

The proposition bet area, as one can see by looking at Figures 3 and 11 has areas to bet such as: 2, 3, 12, 11, 7 and so on. There's no place in that area to bet, for example, 4-1, 3-2, 4-2, 5-1, etc. That is done by making the Hopping bet.

The numbers that one can call out on the Hopping bet are those that are not available in the proposition bet area, such as: 4, 5, 6, 7, 8, 9 and 10, in a specific way. A Hopping bet would generally be made for other arrangements of numbers not shown in this area.

On a dice number 4, one would bet 3-1, Hopping. The Hardway 2-2 is already in the proposition bet area.

On dice number 5, one could bet 4-1 or 3-2 Hopping.

On dice number 6, the Hopping bet would be: 4-2, 5-1. The 3-3 is already in the Hardway area of the proposition bet.

7; There is already a place in proposition bet to bet 7, however, you may bet 7 such as: 6-1, 5-2, or 4-3, Hopping.

On dice number 8, it would be 6-2, 5-3, Hopping. The 4-4 is already on the Hardway portion of the table.

For a dice number 9, it would be 6-3 or 5-4, Hopping.

For dice number 10, one would bet 6-4, Hopping. The 5-5 is already in the Hardway area of the table.

A player can bet the Hardways Hopping also if he would like.

As one may notice, all the Hopping bets have the same odds or probability of occurrence.

In Table I, one can see that all the

Hopping bet arrangements, no matter what the numbers, have two ways in thirty-six of appearing. The odds for this bet would be one in eighteen.

One would also expect the casino to payoff the same for any Hopping bet, and it does. The payoff is the same as the proposition bet Eleven. Note this: It will be a better memory tag than trying to remember all the numbers. The house pays for a Hopping bet, fifteen for one or fourteen to one (same as the Eleven).

The Hopping bet usually has the same limits as the proposition bet area, from about $1 to $500. Some casinos may allow a larger single bet than that; ask!

TECHNICAL STUFF

This is a one roll bet. There are two ways in thirty-six to make any combination of callouts for the Hopping bet. The opportunity to win comes out to be approximately 6%. If any other of the numbers come up, the player loses.

There are thirty-four ways in thirty-six to make any number other than the specific one called for on the Hopping bet. This gives the player about a 94% for loss.

Lays

WHAT'S IT ALL ABOUT?

Complete instructions on how to play the proposition bet on the crap table called, "Lay."

SO WHAT ARE THE PERCENTAGES?

4 or 10 - 17% to win, 8% to lose
5 or 9 - 17% to win, 11% to lose
6 or 8 - 17% to win, 14% to lose

FIGURES AND TABLES

Figure 3, Table V

HOW TO PLAY

When you look at the crap table you will

not see an area designated as a "Lay." This bet is made by the player with the dealer at the player end of the table. It is a Lay against the dice numbers: 4, 5, 6, 8, 9 or 10.

This bet is made when the player feels that all or a particular one of these numbers cannot be made before a 7 appears. If the number is thrown in any combination the player loses. If a 7 appears before the number is thrown the player wins.

The Lay bet costs the player a sizeable investment because he must give or Lay the actual dice number odds plus provide a 5% house profit. If the casino allowed the player to make this bet without laying the odds plus profit the advantage would all be on the player's side.

EXAMPLE

The Lay bet may be made at any time. The player calls a Lay against, let's say, the dice number 4. This is done by giving the chips to the table dealer. He places the chips in the block behind the bordered 4. The dice are thrown. Nothing happens if any number comes up on the dice except for the 4 or a 7. In the event that a 7 appears the player wins and is paid by the table dealer. If the Lay number is thrown in any combination the player loses and the chips are picked up by the table dealer.

DISCUSSION

The Lay bet is not a one roll bet and can

be made at any time. The Lay bet can also be removed at any time without any penalty.

Upon looking at, So What Are the Percentages, the reader may become excited. The percentages are all on the player's side in this game. Over the long run, how could one lose?

The player cannot lose more times than he wins playing the Lay. He can, however, lose more money than he can win here. That's where the casino gets the breaks. Did you believe that they would provide such a great bet area just to see if a player was smart enough to find it?

To make a Lay bet, the player must put up sufficient chips for the bet; the true odds plus a 5% profit on any specific number that he selects to bet. If he wins, he will receive from the dealer an amount equal only to his bet.

How does all of this affect the player? On a game behaving in accordance with the normal mathematical distribution of the dice numbers, the player will win a lot of times but continue to lose 5% plus of his investment capital. Still this is one of the best bets on the craps table. During predictable cold runs of the game it can be a real fortune builder.

If this is such a fair bet, why is it that most players avoid this bet area? There are probably at least two good reasons. First, not many players are familiar with this bet nor its related odds. The second and probably the biggest problem is that it's just too hard for a player to put all that cash on a bet to obtain such a small return. They are used to betting where the payoff is equal to or larger than the original bet.

Another contributing factor is that the largest percentage of crap table players are rarely able to play the don't side of the game even when the table displays long runs of don't side action.

This is not a bet for the small dollar investor. It takes a sizeable bet to obtain the proper 5% for the casino. If one bet anything under $20, then they would be paying even a higher percentage due to the chip denominations.

Table V contains the dice number, true odds and the money relationship for two bet quantities $50 and $100. From this example the player can easily calculate a different value bet. If the player loses, the casino gets all of the invested capital. If the player wins, the casino still retains the profit portion (5%) of the bet.

If a player feels that a dice number 4 will not appear before a 7, and wants to receive a $20 Lay bet against 4, he would Lay bet $40, thereby providing two to one odds plus 5% casino profit of $2. This would be a total investment into that bet of $42. If he wins, $40 of his original investment is returned plus a $20 payoff by the casino.

TECHNICAL STUFF

The Lay bet can be made and removed at any time. Since by observation, dice number 7 seems to appear more often on the shooter's come out roll, the Lay bet might be worthy of

consideration. It could be made just before
the pass line shooter's come out roll and
removed thereafter.

For a better understanding of the odds
arrangement for the Lay bet numbers 4, 5, 6, 8,
9 and 10 refer to the technical stuff portion
of the chapter, THE ODDs, ODDs, & ODDs.

The high quantity of investment capital
required to make the Lay bet does not affect
the percentages of the dice number occurrence.
What it does is require an excessive capital
investment for the low return payoff. These
bets should be utilized only on reasonably
predictable don't side table action.

Dice No.	True Odds	Desired Bet		Lay		5%		Total Bet	
4	2 to 1	50	100	100	200	2	5	102	205
5	3 to 2	50	100	75	150	2	5	77	155
6	6 to 5	50	100	60	120	2	5	62	125
8	6 to 5	50	100	60	120	2	5	62	125
9	3 to 2	50	100	75	150	2	5	77	155
10	2 to 1	50	100	100	200	2	5	102	205

Table V
LAY

THE ODDs, ODDs & ODDs

WHAT'S IT ALL ABOUT?

A complete description on how to play the Odds.

SO WHAT ARE THE PERCENTAGES?

Zero - they are consistent with the probability of the dice number occurrence; whether one takes or places the Odds.

FIGURES & TABLES

Tables II & III

HOW TO PLAY

The Odds may be taken on the Pass Line and

Dice No.	Odds	For Original Bet Of					Pass Line or Come Take Odds Of				
4	2 to 1	1	5	10	20	40	1	5	10	20	40
5	3 to 2	1	5	10	20	40	0	4	10	20	40
6	6 to 5	1	5	10	20	40	0	5	10	20	40
8	6 to 5	1	5	10	20	40	0	5	10	20	40
9	3 to 2	1	5	10	20	40	0	4	10	20	40
10	2 to 1	1	5	10	20	40	1	5	10	20	40

Table II
Taking Odds

Dice No.	Odds	For Original Bet Of					Don't Place Odds Of				
4	2 to 1	1	5	10	20	40	2	10	20	40	80
5	3 to 2	1	5	10	20	40	0	7	15	30	60
6	6 to 5	1	5	10	20	40	0	6	12	24	48
8	6 to 5	1	5	10	20	40	0	6	12	24	48
9	3 to 2	1	5	10	20	40	0	7	15	30	60
10	2 to 1	1	5	10	20	40	2	10	20	40	80

Table III
Placing Odds

come bets. The Odds are placed on the Don't Pass and Don't Come bets.

To take the Odds on the Pass Line, the chips are placed directly behind the Pass Line bet, but outside of the bordered area toward the player's side.

To take the Odds on the Come, the chips are given to the table dealer. He puts the Odds chips on the Come bet.

For the Don't Pass bet, the player places the Odds in the Don't Pass area alongside his original bet and caps it. This is done by placing a portion of the Odds chip stack on both the Odds and original bet.

To place the Odds on the Don't Come, the player gives the money to the table dealer and he does a similar stack in the Don't Come block area behind the numbers.

EXAMPLE

A player has bet on the Pass Line. The shooter has thrown the dice and has obtained a point of 4. The Pass Line bettor would like to take the Odds.

Let's suppose he has a $10 bet on the Pass Line. He would put behind his original bet an Odds bet equal to $10. If the 4 reappeared, he would win. The casino would pay him $10 for his Pass Line bet and $20 for his Odds bet. The total money retrievable by him would be $50. That is a two to one ratio for the Odds bet.

If the player had bet on the Come and the Come point became a 4, he would hand the same

Odds bet to the dealer and would receive the same payoff as the Pass Line.

The Don't Pass bettor for the same point number 4 would place the Odds. This means he must put down chips equal to the actual Odds to receive an additional payoff equal to his original Don't Pass bet. The player would place $20 on the Don't Pass beside his original bet capping $10 of it. Should he win, the casino would pay $10 for his Don't Pass bet and $10 for the Odds bet. The total money available to him is $50 but he has put $30 into the game compared to the Pass Line player $20. The Don't Come action would be exactly the same as the Don't Pass except that the chips would be given to the table dealer. The payoff would also be identical.

DISCUSSION

We have all heard the term, "Odds" associated with most every sporting event. The general meaning of this is that some party has subjectively guessed the outcome arrangement of a football game, basketball game, fight and etc. They have estimated the ratio relationship for such an event and have expressed it in terms of 3 to 1, 2 to 1, or some such ratio.

With the crap game, the Odds are much simpler. They relate directly to probability which can be calculated mathematically. This can be represented as true odds on the probable distribution of the dice cubes numbers over a large quantity of rolls.

In the example of the Pass Line above, it was noted that for the point 4 the player was paid two to one for his Odds bet. This is the actual probability of dice number occurrence. There is a two to one player disadvantage, that is, a 7 to appear before the point number 4. If the player wins, the house pays him the actual true Odds for that Odds portion of the bet; two to one or $20 for the $10 bet.

When taking the Odds, the bet Odds chips are paid with an amount that is equal to the true Odds of the dice. Neither the house nor the player has taken a percentage profit from the Odds bet. This is not true for the original bet; it is paid only in equal sums.

The Odds are placed on the Don't Pass and Don't Come areas of the table. Since the player has the advantage once a point is obtained, he must place the Odds bet equal to the true Odds. Let's look at the same example above only for a Don't point of 4. For a $10 Don't bet, he would have to place a $20 Odds bet giving the casino a two for a possible one payoff. Again, neither the house nor the player takes a percentage profit on the Odds bet.

Table II shows the dice numbers, the true Odds, and what type of Odds may be taken for a corresponding original bet on the Pass Line or Come areas of the dice table.

Table III is for placing the Odds on the Don't Pass and Don't Come areas of the dice table. The numbers are shown as well as the true Odds and the Odds bet required to be placed alongside the original bet.

With a first look at this area, the

perspective player may think that Odds betting
is a real good thing. The house is giving you
the true Odds on the Do side. On the Don't
side you're placing the true Odds. Nobody
takes a percentage.

With a closer look the player will see
that the casino always gets its percentage.
Their percentage is the fact that you have made
the initial Do or Don't side bet to get into
the game. You <u>do not</u> get paid Odds on that
bet. It is only an even money payoff
regardless of the point associated with the
bet. Each player pays his tuition into the
game with the initial Pass Line, Come, Don't
Pass or Don't Come bet.

In taking the Odds on the Do side, the
player may note that his original Pass Line or
Come bet was not adequate to get the proper
Odds. He can, in fact, increase that bet to
any amount and make the corresponding Odds bet
up to the table limit. This is a good thing to
keep in mind for those rare games that become
extremely hot and the player has numerous
passes of the dice.

On the Don't side of the table, if you're
going to place Odds you had better be thinking
ahead, because the casino will not allow you to
add additional chips to the Don't bet in order
to get proper ratios for the Odds
relationship. This takes away from their
percentage of profit in the game.

One should consider the two investment
approaches for the Odds betting. In the case
of taking the Odds on the Do side, the player
puts up an approximate equal investment to his
Pass Line bet. He then gets paid always

something more than the Odds investment for that Odds bet. On the Don't side where the player is placing the Odds, his investment for the Odds runs much greater; as much as twice that of his initial Don't bet. The payoff is always less than his investment in the game.

One should carefully consider placing the Odds on the Don't side because of the quantity of investment capital needed relative to the player's potential betting pool. Placing the Odds is the reverse of taking the Odds.

Looking for a moment at Table II, Taking the Odds, one can see that for a $5 bettor on dice point number 4 or 10, with $5 on the Pass Line, he may take Odds of $5. His payoff would be the true Odds of two to one or $10 for his $5 Odds bet behind the line. In the same case with a dice number of 5 or 9, the Odds are three to two. The player has bet $5 on the Pass Line. He will get paid three for every two that he bets behind the line as Odds. This means he must drop the Odds bet to $4 or increase to $6. Most casinos allow the $6 Odds bet for a $5 Pass Line bet. In the same case, with a dice number of 6 and 8 the bettor bets $5 Odds and gets paid $6.

Smaller bets, for example, a $1 bettor, one can see that when he takes Odds on 4 and 10 he would get paid $2 for the $1 he bets in the Odds. Odds bets of $2 are allowed on 5 or 9 in which he would be paid three for two. For the other numbers: 6 or 8 he will get paid no Odds, if he bet $1 Odds, he would get paid only $1. He could get proper Odds, however, by increasing his Pass Line bet.

This should be kept in mind when making

Odds bets. For placing the Odds the story is reversed.

It is important to point out that if the player is considering taking or placing Odds, that he does some planning before he begins to bet, so that he has the appropriate chips and can make the proper Odds arrangement to maximize his investment. If he does not have the proper chips, he should call the bet out and receive approval from the table dealer until he does get proper chip change.

Some casinos allow players to make double, triple and even 10 times Odds bets. This is nice to know, because through this process there is a definite advantage of collecting large wins and payoffs with only token initial bets. In these cases the casino will allow the player to take Odds which are double, triple, etc., that of his normal original bet.

For a point number of 4 and our example of the $10 bettor; with double Odds the player could put $20 Odds behind the Pass Line, on the triple Odds; he could put $30 Odds behind the Pass Line and etc. His payoff would be still two to one for the Odds. He would get $10 for the Pass Line and $40 for the $20 double Odds bet or $60 for the $30 triple Odds bet.

All of the odds bets (Do or Don't side) may be picked up or called down at any time. If the player gets shaky after making the Odds bets and wants to minimize his investment in the game, then he can pick the Odds chips up off the Pass Line or Don't Pass or call them down on the Come and Don't Come.

For the Come player who has a Come point when the shooter makes his Pass Line point and starts again with a come out roll; the Odds on the Come bet are automatically off for that come out roll. If the come out roll should be a 7, the dealer would pick up the Come chips but he would return the Odds bet chips to the player. The player may call these Odds bets on or working at all times should he choose to do so.

Most casinos have chips with value numbers like $1, $5, $25, $100, $500 and $1000. Tables II and III show the Odds relationship of casinos which have $1 minimum bet and $1 minimum value chips. Some casinos have 25¢ or 50¢ chips. In these cases the player can use the actual chip arrangements for the proper Odds. In casinos where bet chips are 25¢ or 50¢, then taking the Odds for smaller amounts of money can be made more precisely because of the smaller units of chip change.

The Odds on the Pass Line cannot be taken until the shooter establishes a point. If the player puts the Odds bet down early the dealer will tell him to pick it up. On the Come bet, of course, the player must get a Come point number and then the Odds can be taken on that number. The same is true for the Don't Pass; one can't place Odds until they know what point number they are placing the Odds against.

The Odds may be played at any time after that or picked up at any time. The Odds bet doesn't have to be made immediately after the point number is established.

TECHNICAL STUFF

In order to take or place the Odds, the player has to purchase a ticket into the game. This is accomplished by making the original bet on the Pass Line, Come, Don't Pass or Don't Come.

The first and second columns of Tables II and III are identical. The dice Odds numbers are the same whether taking or placing them.

In the Chapter on playing areas of the dice game, the win/loss has been expressed in percentages. It's much easier for someone to calculate percentages than Odds. Odds relate directly to the mathematical calculation of probability and are expressed as a ratio like two to one or 2/1. The chapter, WHAT ABOUT PROBABILITY, completely covers this subject for those interested in pursuing all the details.

The following is a simplified method of developing the Odds from the Table I rather than doing the calculations. From Table I one can see that there are six ways in thirty-six to make a dice number 7.

Considering first the Do side bettor (Pass Line and Come): There are three ways in thirty-six to make the dice number 4 or 10; four ways in thirty-six to make the dice number 5 or 9 and five ways in thirty-six to make a dice number 6 or 8. To express the Odds for the numbers simply do the following:

For 4 or 10: $\dfrac{6 \text{ ways to lose}}{3 \text{ ways to win}}$ or reduce the fraction to 2/1 or two to one.

For 5 or 9: $\dfrac{6 \text{ ways to lose}}{4 \text{ ways to win}}$ or reduce the fraction to 3/2 or three to two.

For 6 or 8: $\dfrac{6 \text{ ways to lose}}{5 \text{ ways to win}}$ or six to five.

The Do side player has a disadvantage in the game of the above ratios. For a 4 or 10 it is twice the chance of losing to winning.

For the Don't side (Don't Pass and Don't Come), one should reverse the ratio of numbers since the player wins when the dice number 7 appears. The numbers are in reality inverted but numerically the same. It would only be confusing for the player to do the conversions and to list them in this manner. They are expressed and understood to be synonymous.

Making the Odds bet adds a larger quantity of money into the game but **does not** change the percentages for the outcome of the game at all, just the payoff. There is no free-ride in the game. The Odds betting is just another way to increase the amount of return on the invested capital, if the player has chosen a winning position.

INSURANCE   TABLE VIII

Area bet	Insurance	Pay off	Note
Pass Line	Any craps C 2, 3&12	8 f 1 8 f 1 30 f 1 15 f 1 30 f 1	+
	Lay point Seven	3/2, 7/5, 7/6 5 f 1	#
Don't Pass	7&11	5f1 15f1	+
	Remove bet Place Point	9/5, 7/5, 7/6	#
Come	Any craps C 2, 3&12	8f1 8f1 30f1, 15f1, 30f1	+
	Lay Point seven	2/1, 3/2, 6/5 5f1	#
Don't Come	7&11	5f1 15f1	+
	Remove bet Place point		#
Place	Remove bet		#
Hardway	Off		+
	Remove bet		#

+ Before Come Out Roll

After Come Out Roll

INSURANCE

WHAT'S IT ALL ABOUT?

Everybody has insurance for everything - why not for gambling?

FIGURES AND TABLES

Table VIII

DISCUSSION

Most of us protect against sudden loss by insuring our autos, houses, jewelry, airplanes and etc. Although expensive, insurance allows one some peace of mind knowing that our material investment will be protected.

Rarely is one able in the business world to insure against the loss of an investment. With certain types of investments this can be accomplished, but in general, one cannot procure insurance on investment capital.

It would be nice if one could obtain insurance for the investment bets made at the dice table. As it turns out, this is a possibility. The system has to be understood to make this insurance possible.

When we insure anything, we pay an insurance premium. This premium is expensive, but we consider it worthwhile compared to the overall sudden loss. With the craps table, the same type of premium expense exists to insure our bets.

If one were to purchase a new auto and obtain the premium cost of full insurance coverage. Then take the equivalent amount of money and deposit it into a money market account. He should deposit it in the same manner that one would pay the insurance premium. It turns out that in about 8 years the money invested in this manner would equal an amount about the same as the purchase price of the car.

Not all areas of the table can be insured. Through some reconstruction of the playing rules and procedures; this text contains an insurance plan that one can use to insure the major crap table areas.

In the Insurance Table VIII, there are bet areas such as Pass Line, Don't Pass, Come, Don't Come, Place and Hardway. This table shows when and how to obtain insurance in each of these areas. This can be accomplished by looking at this table for the bet area (left column) and the insurance option (next column).

Let's look at an example of insuring a

Pass Line bet: The Pass Line would lose on the come out roll if craps 2, 3 or 12 were thrown. To insure against that loss one could bet Any Craps, "C" or the individual numbers 2, 3 and 12. The amount bet would have to be appropriate to cover the amount that the player has as an original Pass Line bet.

For example, if one bet (invested) $10 on the Pass Line and bet $1 on Any Craps then his payoff would be, eight for one or $7. He would be short $3 in getting the original $10 investment back. However, he would have protected against the major loss. If he wanted to over-insure he could bet $2 or Any Craps. This would bring him a return of $14 and a profit of $4 should the craps appear. In this case the cost for insurance is 20% of the invested capital.

One can judge how much insurance he may procure based upon whether he would want to insure against major or all losses.

Once the point is established on a Pass Line, the other portion of the second column contains methods to protect against loss. Insurance gets more expensive here. If one were to lay against the point, insurance would cost more than the original bet on the Pass Line. One would have to be quite sure of his intuitive feelings and be certain that the game was going sour; that the shooter would not make the point.

To bet 7 is a little easier since the payoff is five for one. If one had the same $10 pass line bet and became concerned he could bet $2 on the 7 and if his guess was right he would get his $10 back with only a 20%

insurance cost.

The Come area is identical to the Pass Line in the methods of insurance. One can see that for the same condition, the same example above would prevail here also.

For the Don't Pass bet, on the come out roll, if the shooter throws a 7 or 11, the player loses. From Table VIII it can be seen that he can bet 7 and 11 in proper multiples to cover his losses. Once the point is established the Don't Pass player may remove his bet without any penalty. He might consider doing that. If he feels he is up against a strong shooter who will make the point, he could place bet the Pass Line point while leaving the Don't Pass bet alone and pick up some profit should the Pass Line shooter make the point. This type of bet is of little value. It is strictly observation protection of capital loss. It's much better to pick up the bet.

The Don't Come area is identical to the Don't Pass area for the insurance portion except that to remove the bet one would have to tell the dealer to remove the bet. Whereas on the Don't Pass Line the bet can be removed at any time by the player.

For a place bet, just call the bet off. The place bets can be called off/down at any time. They are not working during the come out roll unless the player requests it. This eliminates the come out roll risk. If the player wants insurance he tells the dealer to remove the bet. That removes all of his capital risk.

If one has a bet on the Hardway during the

come out roll he would normally call the bet
off. That protects against a 7 on a come out
roll. Once the shooter has established a
point, the Hardway bets are like the place
bets, the bet can be removed by telling the
stickman to either take your bet off or take
your bet down. When he takes your bet off, he
just leaves the bet in the Hardway area. It is
not working for whatever amount of rolls you
would wish it not to work. In the case of
calling the bet down, he would withdraw the bet
and have the dealer pay you that amount.

The reason that the remaining bets such as
Field and the Proposition areas are not shown
with methods to insure them is that they are
one roll bets. While there are ways to insure
them, one would be betting, for and against, at
the same time. There is little gain to get
paid in one area and lose in another area.

HOW TO WIN

WHAT'S IT ALL ABOUT?

Winning? Who wins? Who loses? Why? See if your style is contained herein.

DISCUSSION

What is winning? Winning is taking a larger (numerically higher) value of bet chips IN from the game than you're putting OUT into the game. Anyone could have said that; everyone knows that.

This may sound simplistic, but is it really? Should it not be the objective of the player interested in winning at the crap table to attempt to put more chips in his rail than he's leaving on the table?

What about the quantity of chips he puts in his rail? Is it not better to win $100, $500 or etc., and still win than to lose $200, $300 or $1000? Must one always win big or lose big? An accumulation of small consistent wins like a small profit from many businesses will ultimately provide the player with a large win (See the chapter, Invest Don't Gamble).

Losing on the other hand is a simple matter of the reverse process in which more chips leave the rail into the game than the player is picking up from the game.

Who are the winners and who are the losers anyway? Is the winner the one who has the luck and the loser the one who has lost his luck for the day? If that's the belief of the player then he is going to have to attain a change of philosophy and attitude.

Who wins? Does the winner always win? Is it important that he always win? Rarely in life is anything 100% as far as winning. If one were in business he may not expect every day that he would make enough to cover his overhead. The few days of the month that he does do big business is when he not only covers his overhead but obtains his profit.

It's not necessary to win in each game. It is necessary if you're going to stay in the winning circle to win. Keep track of the wins and losses, and over some given selected period of time; an hour, day, week, month or year, the player must show a profit to be a winner.

WINNING BUT NOT KNOWING IT

If a player on the craps table had a stack of chips and they disappeared over an hour or so of play he would normally think that he was actually losing. He may be winning.

When we equilibrate the game accounting

for the probability, it may be interesting for the player to see that he may have indeed been winning. How can this happen? The player could be losing less than he would be expected to lose in the game because of house percentages based upon the statistical probability of the dice numbers occurrence.

The casino attempts to keep the dice rolling across the table at a very rapid pace. It only makes sense that if there are more rolls, there are more numbers and more numbers increases the amount in which the house can absorb from the players in any particular unit of time. (Casino percentage on each number times the rate of number flow).

On tables where there are few players and uncomplicated type of bets, the dice will roll ten or more times per minute. This is once each six seconds or so.

On tables where the dealers have a lot of complicated bets and payoffs, the roll rate may be slowed down to as few as two per minute or thirty seconds between rolls.

To illustrate this game concept, let's take an example where the average is approximately five rolls per minute. The dice would be rolled each twelve seconds. Let's consider that the player is a $10 passline and $10 basic unit bettor. Assume that the player bets $10 on the passline and $10 on odds or elsewhere. He, of course, could be betting more than that elsewhere if he is betting $10 with each roll action. In this example, however, he makes only these two bets.

Using the statistical base, after each six rolls one would expect a dice number 7 to appear and a change of action. This would give the player fifty actions per hour at $20 per action or a $1,000 an hour cash flow in the game.

Now depending on the point numbers and the play areas that are obtained, he should expect a 3% to 22% disadvantage and would lose from $30 to $220 per hour. This is due to the long run statistical percentages. It is the edge that the casino has built into the crap table operation.

If at the end of an hour's play the player is even or down a few dollars, then he has obviously been winning. The player can count his bet amounts and determine his actual cash flow at the table. He can then equate his status based upon the equilibrated position in the game and not just by the quantity of chips remaining in the rail.

This provides little comfort for the player interested in winning real dollars. It does point out that the player who walks away from the table a $500 winner, who has played several hours, has indeed won in equilibrated dollars probably double or triple that amount.

The player should be able to see from this example that if he bets every play in the game, using the same bet quantity on every roll of the dice, and stays in the game for some extended period of time, then his funds will be absorbed by the casino's profit edge.

The two important points of this discussion are that: The player should not necessarily bet each and every play of the dice unless he's winning on each bet. Secondly, if he's going to consistently win he must vary the

amount of his bet in order to increase the
investment and the rate of return, when
winning, to compensate for the loss periods.

It's quite apparent that the player who
bets the same amount of money on every roll of
the dice will have his funds consumed by the
casino. However, if it's any comfort to one
who has been able to hang in there for a long
time he can calculate and relate to his friends
how much he has won in equilibrated dollars.

The Casino Edge

The casino depends upon these factors for
their profit:
1.   They have the long term statistical
percentage in the game.
2.   The public lacks understanding and
knowledge of the game.
3.   Pattern bettors; most players are habitual
mammals and will always bet the same way, same
pattern. It's only a matter of time until the
dice number percentages overwhelm the player's
capital capability.
4.   Psychological factors
        a) Ego of player believing he can change
            the game.
        b) Fear of winning
            It's easy to lose, no more stress,
            the money's gone.
            Dependence of luck for a win, not
            knowledge.
        c) Impatience - player will tire of
            playing and try for one big push and
            eventually will lose it all.
        d) Rush to bet; a player not sure of what

to bet will rush to put chips on the table usually in an easy high risk area.

e) Bet big when losing and bet little while winning.

f) The player won't quit when ahead, just when he is broke.

g) Inflexible playing patterns. He will win his way or else.

h) Inability of player to have knowledge of or be able to detect runs. He will revert to pass line and come dreams.

i) Player expects or unconsciously wants to lose.

5) Environment

a) Player awed by plush casino surroundings.

b) Acceptance of freebies, like drinks (too many).

c) Player feels charitable or intimidated by the casino.

6) Give the player anything he wants, all the freedom to beat himself - he will - the casino never beats the player, he always beats himself.

7) The casino has many management tools to control hot tables. Among them are:

a) Slow down the game to less rolls per unit of time.

b) Friendly intimidation by suggesting that the shooter:

1. Shoot the dice as soon as he gets them.

2. Dice must hit the opposite end of the table.

3. Try to throw the dice down the

center of the table.
4. Shoot them harder, softer, and etc.
c) More frequent visits of the cocktail
waitress.

Past experience has proven these techniques rattle the shooter and other players about the tables. Stay aloof, don't let anyone rattle your cage.

Who Loses? Why?

Why does one lose? Does one lose simply because he doesn't understand what is happening with the game; doesn't have a full working knowledge of the entire game? In many cases this is the difference between a winner and a loser.

Is the loser inflexible, unable to bet according to the observed action on the table? Is he bullheaded? Is he incapable of observing the run trends? Does he know what type of bet to make when he is able to determine trends? Is he a winner, ahead in the game, but does not know when to quit?

Does he gamble drunk, tired, fatigued and not too alert? Does he make improper investments into the game for the expected results of any bet? Does he rush to bet without having any idea of what's happening in the game? When he begins to lose, does he bet heavily on the down side and then as wins occur begin to back off from making the proper size bets?

Anyone who's played a few games of dice has probably experienced one or more of these feelings.

Man seems to have a unique inbred ability to become set on undertaking the difficult, near impossible, destructive tasks. The deeper one gets into these tasks, the more intent and determined becomes the drive. It encompasses a realm of tunnel vision; almost an obsession to succeed. While this phenomena may serve man well in some areas of endeavor. It usually does not work well in gambling.

Winning

Can one win at the dice game? Answer: YES. Can one win on every craps game play on any table? Probably not.

The best bets are removable bets where the player can make instant decisions and can operate freely. These are:

Place	Don't Pass
Hardways	Don't Come
Lays	

Anybody can play at this game, but if one wants to be a winner, he is going to have to know this game. He must know the rules for each area of play. In addition, knowledge of the following chapters is a must to be a consistent winner: The ODD's, ODD's & ODD's; INSURANCE; BETTING SYSTEMS, HERE'S MORE; AN EXPERT ON YOUR FIRST TRIP; DO's & DONT's; CRAP TABLE OPERATION; AH! YES, THE CASINO; THAT SILLY CUBE; WHO'S MANAGING THE MONEY; THE CRYSTAL BALL and INVEST, DON'T GAMBLE.

Runs, what are they, how do they happen, why are they so important? Some type of runs are occurring during most of the dice game play time. What are they? They are group or arrangements of number occurrence not in concert with the standard expected mathematical statistics of the game. They may appear as four craps in a row, $1 bet parlayed would result in a $512 win, three dice number 12 in a row, $1 bet parlayed into $27,000, three 11's in a row, $1 bet could be parlayed into $3,375, five 7's in a row, ten rolls of field numbers, thirty rolls of dice numbers without the appearance of a 7. Five dice number 9's in a row, eight don't pass hands in a group, Eleven Pass line hands in a group, five hardway 6's over a few rolls, and etc., etc. It can be an exciting game just looking for and identifying these runs, but it gets even more fun when one has committed a wager to the run theory. Why do they happen? What are the cause factors? Who knows, furthermore, who cares? These runs can be identified and used as tools in our investment portfolio. Science has never quantified gravitation. They have footprinted its characteristics, defined it mathematically and make use of it as a tool. Why are runs so important to the player? Accurate identification and proper betting of runs is a devistation to the casino. They worry much about this problem. While the casino has the long term statistical profit percentages all on their side, they can't do a thing about the runs. The runs are the player's diamond in the most polished form. It's the power tool in the player's hands that the casino can't touch. If all the players took advantage of these runs using proper bets the casino could not stay in business. They could not stay in a profit position. Polish the technique of identifying and making proper bets on many different types of runs that are constantly occurring and one will have found the real key to the casino's gold mine.

The worst table to play at is one that has long periods of undefinable runs. The one up, one down scene is bad news. If one can't define some movement and get on it, he can't win. Fortunately, these conditions only exist for short periods at most dice table games. If one can recognize such a game, take a break or consider moving to another table.

Keep periods of play short. Long enough to feel comfortable in the game but not so long as to become, ho-hum bored. Move on to another table, put some interesting variety into your life, you'll do better.

One should not get hung up on bullheaded pursuit. Be smart, back off and view the threshold gain or loss from such a venture. Shift into neutral until a reasonable direction and course can be charted.

Patience is not a virtue in this game, it's a must. One must be able to observe what is occurring. He must then spring on it as if he were a tiger, observing and calculating the precise moment to make the move upon his prey where his chances for success are maximized and his prey's (the casinos) chances for escape are minimized.

Take some time out to introduce yourself to you. Try to spend some time with your forever buddy, you. The better you get to know him, the more fruitful both of your lives will be. If you can realistically get to understand his motives in gaming as well as his emotional reactions under the play conditions then you can both work at correcting the discipline and control deficiencies. This will help promote growth into the winning circle.

When does one quit? This is the biggest question of all. The inability to resolve this individual question can and does convert the natural winner into a loser. One must tackle and put the question to rest or he'll never win even when he does. Each one must find his own way to accomplish this task. Here is one suggested solution:

Winning - after each successful thrust of new profits establish a 25% of winnings loss/limit. If one hasn't obtained a new surge of winnings and profits by the time he has invested this 25% back into the game, quit. Pack up the tent and camel and go have some fun with your winnings.

Losing - establish a loss/limit pool for play. If one begins to play and never reaches a win position, i.e., the income from the game has not increased the quantity of the pool to greater than the initial pool, then quit when the loss/limit pool is exhausted. Take a break for several hours, days, or. If the losing player enters a winning position before exhaustion of the loss/limit pool follow the instructions for winning above. Being a winner is much more fun than the converse and being a winner on 90% of the game entries should be the player's goal.

Not winning? If what one is doing isn't working, try something else. Keep trying until you're in tune with what's really going on in the game. This is an offensive game. One cannot win this war by being able to defend his borders. The house' percentage battalion can eventually penetrate any player defense, no matter how clever one may think it is. The winning player must always be training and dispatching his best offensive teams to hit the momentarily defenseless casino gold mines.

Get excited about life! Especially at CRAPS, it helps. Find fun in everything. It's there, all one has to do is look with eyes that see and senses that perceive to find it. If one wakes up and says, "Life's a drag, another dung day, living sucks, I know before the day's over some excretion is going to dump on me and make it even worst," then his operational forte is questionable. He's probably become engaged in a big inward self pity circle jerk, poor baby. He doesn't need his five or six senses, isn't using them, anyway. If one is in such a mood, he would do far better to stay away from the casino until it passes.

Studies show that the best way to maximize the bet areas relative to the run phenomena is as follows:

*Pass Line - Consider place bet instead, bet per Table Xa or bet, press, drag one half, use drag for odds or profit as desired, continue to alternate using press, then one half drag.

*Don't Pass - Bet per Table Xa or bet, press, drag one half, do not place odds, continue to alternate the press followed by drag of one half.

*Field - Bet per Table Xa, Table XI, field/place combo or bet, press, drag one half, continue to alternate pressing and then dragging one half.

Come - Don't play, use the place bet instead, it has better player percentages and can be removed when desired.

Don't Come - Bet per Table Xa or make two or three bets immediately after the shooter's come out roll, consider no action on 6 and 8, call bets down if concerned, double amount to replace lost bet. Do not place odds.

Big 6 & 8 - Don't play, use the place bet 6 & 8 instead, get better player percentages 7 for 6 versus even money on Big 6 & 8.

*Place Bets - start by making one to three bets on numbers that are appearing, press or spread funds to other numbers when they hit. Alternate the press, drag or spread techniques. Don't hesitate to shift bets from one number to the next, if desired.

Seven - Table Xb.

Horn - Bet only if desired. It's better to bet any craps and eleven or individually bet the specific numbers.

Hardways - Table Xc or Xd or use parley method.

Any Craps - Table Xg or parley winnings for two to three hits.

2 & 12 - Table Xf or parley winnings for two hits.

Eleven - Table Xe or parley winnings for two to four hits.

Hopping - Pull winnings down when bet hits.

*Lays - On come out roll for new shooter. Immediately, against the point on weak shooter or cold tables.

      * Do not hesitate to pull all possible funds down at anytime if you get that feeling.

When re-entering the game after a pull down, bet with the quantity that was up before the removal.

Quitting power - The player can quit any time he pleases. He has no time/play contract with the casino. On the other hand, the casino can't quit and go home. They must keep playing no matter what is happening.

If you think you have time on your hands, you're wrong. The advantage element of time is always in the casino's hands.

Assume you're going to be wrong on more bets than you'll be right. Who cares? You can still win if you are right on several consecutive bets and you bet properly.

Always token bet when wrong. As consecutive wins begin to occur no matter where you're betting, always drag some funds to increase your profit and investment pool and increase your investment (bet) in the game.

If you start betting near the house maximum quantity bet limit, you will lose the edge because you can't increase your bet as consecutive wins occur to take advantage of the consecutive win process.

No two games are the same. Applied historical knowledge doesn't work well; don't get hung up on history studies. The player must know what's happening now and realistically predict the future rolls.

Maintain emotional stability - Get tough - it's only a game, it's nothing important like health, love, etc. Hope is for dreamers. If you want to dream a big win do it in your bed, it's cheaper. If you're easily discouraged or depressed, then play with dolls, don't play craps. Get the kind of doll that cries, then you can have someone to share tears with. Don't be a happy loser. A happy loser is a fool.

Don't try to fight the house percentage - they have it - if you're working on a 3% house profit you will last longer than if you're working on a 22%, but it's still only a matter of time before your capital pool becomes their profit. Don't buck the system. Go with the flow, only use it to your advantage. Take advantage of the runs in progress.

90% of the game time you should be making token bets and exercising your brain asking questions like: What's happening? What were the past rolls? What will the future rolls be? What's really happening here? What type of runs are in progress? In less than 10% of the table time is where you will make all the money.

If you're playing at the tables and don't know what's happening then you should go take your naps where they provide pillows. They don't have these at the casino tables.

If one could always pick the proper moves in the winning bet area at the right time, he would win on each bet. There would be no need for this book. The player could simply bet as much as he wants to win. Statistically we know that this is impossible.

It's not necessary to win on each play in order to win over all. When one wins, he should win big. When one loses it should be small. That's the opposite of what the casino expects from the player.

The casino expects a player to win in

dollars and lose in hundreds and thousands of dollars. The player needs to reverse his thinking on this process and win in hundreds and thousands of dollars and lose in dollars.

Each time a winner charges forward he should cover yards toward the goal zone. If he takes momentary setbacks they should be in distances of feet. The overall movement is one of forward mobility. A winner never gets caught up in the trap of a single giant movement backwards.

BETTING SYSTEMS, HERE'S MORE

WHAT'S IT ALL ABOUT?

A systems approach to making bets as favorable runs of dice numbers begin to occur.

DISCUSSION

One of the saddest things that anyone could observe at the craps game is to see someone who is involved in an exceptionally good run of dice number wins and to see them making only token quantity bets throughout the entire run. The game may go through 10 to 15 passes of the dice and the player will win only a few dollars.

If this player would have used any reasonable betting system or would have been aware of such systems, he could have parlayed his wins into hundreds or thousands of dollars with virtually no risk at all.

The betting systems presented here are not systems to beat the odds of the game. There is no foolproof way to beat the odds. The odds of this game always favor the casino.

What these betting systems do is to allow one an orderly way to extend the investment capital pool. As the bets begin to pay off, it allows a complete return plus profit on the invested capital.

Sometimes you see gamblers that are doing very well at making consecutive bets that pay off. They are in tune with the table events and making good location bets. The problem is that they're not making the proper bet amounts to make any money. It's kind of like an employee being too busy working to make any money.

The player that consistently makes the money is one who is thinking a little ahead of the game. As the consecutive bets begin to pay off he finds a way to get the edge on the game. As one becomes accurate at making bets that pay off, he needs to expand the bet investment quantity.

The systems presented here extend the time in which the player can lose before he hits a win and still leave him in fairly good shape to continue wagering.

This text presents systems for each major area of the crap table. General discussion and reference for each are described in this chapter.

DOUBLE UP METHOD

The Double Up Method of betting in theory

is an excellent idea since it's impossible to lose. In practicality it takes on another face, one that can lead to big loses.

In the Double Up Method the individual bets twice what he just lost until he wins. When he wins, he will always win an amount equal to the initial unit of his original bet. This is then his net win. The Double Up Method always leaves the bettor ahead. However, in reality, one using the Double Up Method will rapidly run into trouble.

Table IX shows the Double Up Method. In viewing this table it's easy to see how rapidly the bets expand into a large capital investment. The real problem is that one soon reaches the casino table limit of 500; 1,000; 2,000 or whatever it may be. He then can only bet that limit amount and he loses the edge provided by the Double Up Method. The other problem is that few gamblers have sufficient cash or credit, even if there was not a table limit, to use this method.

In Table IX, one can see that the bet begins with 1 then 2, 4, 8, 16, 32, 64, 128. The table stops at 128, but the individual can continue the process. The losses are shown in the third column. The amount that one would win is in the fourth column and the last column shows the profit/loss. With the Double Up Method one is always ahead one unit. The one unit being the initial unit bet made by the player.

Let's take an example of the Double Up Method: suppose one was playing the passline and bet $1. The bet is $1. If he wins, he wins $1 which makes the total win in front of him $2. His net profit is $1. Now, if he loses, he bets $2. If he loses again it's $4, $8, $16, $32, $64 and $128. This table may be used for all bets. It is a unit table. The player may simply multiply the unit value in columns two, three, four and five by his unit bet.

Suppose the player has $10 as a unit bet. Column two would be $10; the loss would be $10, if he lost it. A win would be $20, but his net profit/loss would be a plus $10. If he loses then he doubles, that's 2 x $10 or $20. The rest of the chart is multiplied the same way. If he loses again, he bets 4 x $10 or $40. If he loses again, it's 8 x $10 or $80. If again he loses, it's 16 x $10 or $160, and etc. The table is used in the same manner no matter what the bet may be. Simply multiply the unit bet by numbers appearing in the columns two, three, four and five.

Some players like the Double Up Method. It, however, seems unrealistic to play this method since the investment funds required become large very fast and there's little chance of recouping. If one does win, he's winning a small amount for the large amount that is risked.

A better method would be to use Table Xa. This allows the player an opportunity to win over many rolls with less capital invested.

The Double Up Method of betting may be used on any area of the table that pays even money such as Pass, Don't Pass, Come, Don't Come and Field (for numbers other than the double or triple numbers 2 & 12).

PROGRESSIVE BETTING

The Progressive Betting allows the player to extend his capital pool, increasing it and increasing his investment in the game, while minimizing his risks. These methods are preferred over the Double Up Method because of the lower quantities of capital resources required for the game play.

TABLE Xa

Where used: Any area that pays even money for a bet. Pass, Don't Pass, Come, Don't Come, Big 6, Big 8, & Field.

This table does not account for players taking the odds. It is for the basic unit bet. The corresponding odds, if taken, would add to the required capital and are not shown in this table.

Table Xa is used by a player who is making token unit bets until wins occur. Whenever he is not winning he makes only a unit bet of any value ($1, $10, $100, or whatever). The table begins as the first win occurs.

On the leftmost column is the roll/bet number after the first win. The second column is the action, what the player would actually do. The third column is the bet that's left on the table. The fourth column shows instantaneous profit and loss. The last column shows what one would have accumulated, if on that roll instead of betting he took all the chips off the table.

One can see by the fifth consecutive win that the player has 5 units bet. He has a 2 unit profit and a 7 unit drag all profit. On the 10th consecutive bet, he's now at a 40 unit bet, a 43 unit profit and an 83 unit drag all position.

Table Xa is designed for the player who has consecutive wins. It matters not whether they are on the Pass, Don't Pass, switch bet or whatever as long as he's right, consecutively right.

One can see that if he made 20 consecutive proper bets using this table he would have a profit of 2,043 units or a drag all profit of 2,543 units. If the player was betting a $1 unit, he would win $2,043 as shown. If he is a $10 unit bettor there would be $20,430 that the player would have won.

DOUBLE, DRAG

This contains a conservative approach to betting the even payoff areas of the table. Some players may prefer, as wins occur, to make bets such as DOUBLE then DRAG, Double, Drag, Double, Drag as a continuing process. This method keeps doubling the investment into the game. There is a little more capital at risk. It does, however, provide a more rapid return and investment into the game. It's also easy to remember; no tables to memorize.

TABLE Xb

Where used: This is for proposition bet area Seven.

This system should be played on cold tables where there's no long extended runs of numbers. It should also be used when one intuitively feels that the end of a shooter's cycle is over. It may be used for insurance protecting on Don't Pass and Don't Come bets.

If one attemped to bet Seven on a table having a long run number shooter, he would soon reach the loss limit.

When the player hits and receives a payoff, he should call the entire bet down and start at the beginning of the table again when he desires any further betting. The player can stop the bet cycle at any place. He would keep track of his last bet quantity, if he terminates the cycle. Later he can continue betting and increasing his bet until he hits a payoff just as he would when betting consecutively.

The leftmost column of Table Xb is the roll number. The second column is the amount bet. The third column is the amount of the accumulated loss. The fourth column is the amount of a instant win and the last column is the net win. This is the accumulated loss minus the win.

Let's suppose that a player has bet eight times before he gets a win. At roll 8 his bet is $4, he would have an accumulated loss of $17 and he would have won $20 which gives him a net win of $3.

Refer to proposition bet area "Seven" for all the rules associated with betting this area.

The table Xb allows for eleven rolls which is almost double the expected normal distribution of the dice.

This is a unit bet table, if one is betting some other unit bet, say $5 instead of

$1, simply multiply all numbers by 5.

Table Xc

Where used: For Hardway 6 & 8 bets.

The Hardway 6 & 8 bets should be made when there is a frequent occurrence of these Hardways numbers. Hardway number runs quite often do appear. See the appropriate chapter on how to play the proposition bet area, "Hardway 6 & 8."

The left column is the roll or bet number. The next column is the actual bet the player would be making. The third column from the left is the loss the player would suffer. It is the accumulated loss at that point in the game. The fourth column is the amount the player would win. The last column is the net amount the player would win. This is the accumulated win minus the loss.

Each time the player bets and loses, he would continue to bet according to the next row down the table. If he won, then he would drag all and revert to the top line of the table to begin the cycle over again.

It is very unlikely that a player could lose on Hardway 6 & 8 using this progressive bet table. This Table Xc allows the player thirty-nine bets which is about four times the statistical odds for occurrence.

This is a unit bet table, if the player is betting some other unit bet, say $10 instead of $1, then he would simply multiply the numbers in the last four columns by 10.

TABLE Xd

Where used: When betting Hardway 4 and 10.

The Hardways should be bet when it is observed that Hardway number runs are in progress. See the chapter, HOW TO PLAY, for instructions on playing this area.

The left column of the table is the consecutive roll or bet number. The second column is the actual bet. The third column is the accumulated loss. The fourth column is the instant win amount. The last column is the net win which is the accumulated loss, minus the instant win.

If one bets $1, the play is exactly as portrayed in the table. If one bet $10 then everything would be multiplied by 10. If the player bet $1 and lost on the first bet, then he would move to the second bet which is $1 and so on. Suppose he's now at the tenth consecutive bet without a win. On this attempt he has bet $3, his accumulated loss is $16 and his win is $24, leaving him a net win of $8. Once the player has won, he would revert back to the beginning of the table and start the process all over again if desired.

HARDWAY PARLEY

The Hardway Parley method is for betting any or all of the hardway numbers. To do this bet, say $1, on Hardway 4. When Hardway 4 hits, simply say, "Parley." Continue this process for as long as your good judgement or nerves can hold out. If you lose, you have lost only $1.

When you win, your bet goes to $8 or $10, $64 or $100, $512 or $1000, then $4096 or

$10,000 depending upon which hardway number is bet. Quit anywhere that you wish. Not a bad approach for only the risk of one little dollar.

TABLE Xe

Where used: When making proposition bets 3 or 11.

Proposition bet area 3 or 11 may be made during a comeout roll of the dice or at anytime the player feels that these numbers are about to occur in runs.

The first column in the table is the roll number. The second column is the actual bet units. The third column is the accumulated loss units. The fourth column is the instant win quantity. The last column is the net win. This is the instant win minus the accumulated loss units.

Suppose that the player has been playing 3 and he's bet eleven times without a win. On his twelfth bet, one can see that the bet is 2 units. The loss, should it occur, would be an accumulated 14 units. The win, should it occur, 30 units and the net win would be 16 units.

This table is identical for use on either 3 or proposition bet 11. Once the win occurs, the player would drag all and begin at the top line of the table with any further bets.

See the proposition bet area "3 and 11" in the chapter, HOW TO PLAY, for an understanding of the playing rules for this area.

This is a unit bet table, if the player is betting some other value, say $10 instead of $1, then he would simply multiply the numbers in the last four columns by 10.

TABLE Xf

Where used: For making proposition bets 2
or 12.

This four page table is for betting either
2 (snake eyes) or 12 (box cars).

The table is divided by a horizontal line
at each change in unit bet size. This table
would be used where the player feels that runs
of 2 or 12 are occurring in the game or at any
other time the player thinks these numbers
could appear.

The leftmost column contains the roll or
bet number. The second column contains the bet
quantity.   The third column contains the
accumulated unit bet loss. The fourth column
contains the instant unit bet win. The last
column contains the net win. This is the win
minus the accumulated loss.

This Table Xf allows for 128 consecutive
bets. This is approximately three and one-half
times the normal expected dice number
distribution.

The player should refer to the chapter,
HOW TO PLAY, for information on playing the
proposition bet "2 & 12."

This is a unit bet table, if the player is
betting some other value, say $10 instead of
$1, then he would simply multiply the numbers
in the last four columns by 10.

TABLE Xg

Where used: When playing proposition bet

area, Any Craps.

The chapter, HOW TO PLAY, should be referred to for information on playing the proposition bet area, "Any Craps."

This area should be bet when the player feels that runs of craps are going to appear. It also may be used as insurance for Pass and Come bets.

The player would make each consecutive bet as shown in the table until a win occurs. He would then drag all and revert back to the beginning of the table.

The left column is the roll or bet number. The next column is the bet quantity in units. The third column is the accumulated loss. The fourth column is the instant win and the last column is the net win which is the instant win minus the accumulated loss.

Let's suppose that the player has bet Any Craps five times and has not won. He would begin his sixth bet on the table (6th line down). The bet unit quantity would be 2. The loss, if that roll became a loss, would be 7 units. The win, if he won on that roll, would be 16 units. The net win, should he win, would be 9 units.

If the player is a $1 unit bettor he would bet directly as shown.

This is a unit bet table, if the player is betting some other value, say $10 instead of $1, then he would simply multiply the numbers in the last four columns by 10.

TABLE XI

Where used: When playing the Field/Place

combo.

One may refer to the chapter, HOW TO PLAY, to understand the playing areas of the "Field" and the "Place Bet."

The system of making combination bets on the Field and certain Place Bets allows one to cover the game so that one will receive a payoff on every roll that may occur on the table with the exception of the dice number 7. This is an interesting betting arrangement in that one is getting action on each roll of the dice.

This is accomplished by betting the Field which contains all numbers except for the 5, 6, 7 and 8. Then covering these numbers by place betting the 5, 6 and 8. Of course, if the 7 appears it is a loss across the board.

If one tried to cover this by also betting proposition bet 7, it would make the system unbalanced. One would be putting more into the game than it would return to the player, so one must suffer the 7 risk.

This should be played during times when a shooter is having a long roll of the dice where a variety of numbers come up, but definitely a run in which a 7 does not appear.

Table XI shows the relationship of the Field and the place bet payoffs. If a dice number 2 appears, the Field pays a minimum of two to one. Sometimes it pays triple or more but the minimum in all casinos is two to one. If a 3 appears, it pays even chips. A 4 pays even. A 5 would lose on the Field but win on the place bet 5 with a payoff of seven for five or 140%. The same with the 6 & 8 except the payoff is seven for six or 120%. A 9, 10 & 11 would win in the Field and pay even chips. A 12 would pay a minimum of two to one in the Field and at some casinos triple.

In this combination bet the Field pays off but the place bets do not lose. When the place bets pay off, however, the Field does lose. A portion of the place bet payoff has to be returned to replace the Field bet loss.

Bet unit quantities are not listed here simply because the player may select his own depending on the minimum bet limits of that dice table. Most casinos have a $5 minimum bet. It would then be necessary to use a minimum bet of $5. To place bet 5 would be $5, place bet 6 would be $6 and place bet 8 would be $6. The Field would require a $5 minimum bet.

Some casinos allow smaller quantities for place bets. In that case this amount can be reduced if the player desires to do so. It can also be increased by multiples of 5 and 6. In other words, one could bet $10 on 5, and $12 on the 6 & 8 or any multiples of $5 and $6 upwards.

This bet arrangement requires a larger initial cash outlay. At most casinos a minimum is required of $5 in the Field, $5 on the 5, $6 on the 6 and $6 on the 8. This a total of $22.

If the player is incorrect in estimating the runs of the table, a 7 may appear and all would be lost in one sweep. If the player is correct, however, when long runs of scattered numbers occur, the money accumulates very rapidly.

The player should increase the bet as he gains a good rail chip position. He should increase his bet on the table and continue this process of dragging chips then increasing the table investment. It is possible to begin with only $22 and end up winning several thousand dollars in just a few minutes betting this Field/Place combination.

To do so, the player must increase his bets. A preferred system would be to double the bets each time the player has accumulated a gain in amount of the risked money on the table.

Prior to Roll No.	Bet	Loss	Win	Hit Profit + Loss −
1	1	1	2	+1
2	2	3	4	+1
3	4	7	8	+1
4	8	15	16	+1
5	16	31	32	+1
6	32	63	64	+1
7	64	127	128	+1
8	128	255	256	+1

Table IX
Double-Up

Prior to Roll No.	Action	Bet	Profit + Loss −	Drags all Profit
1	——————	1	−1	——————
2	Drag 1	1	0	1
3	" 0	2	0	2
4	" 1	3	+1	4
5	" 1	5	+2	7
6	" 2	8	+4	12
7	" 3	13	+7	20
8	" 6	20	+13	33
9	" 10	30	+23	53
10	" 20	40	+43	83
11	" 20	60	+63	123
12	" 30	90	+93	183
13	" 60	120	+153	273
14	" 90	150	+243	393
15	" 100	200	+343	543
16	" 100	300	+443	743
17	" 100	500	+543	1043
18	" 500	500	+1043	1543
19	" 500	500	+1543	2043
20	" 500	500	+2043	2543

Table Xa

Roll	Bet	Loss	Win	Net Win
1	1	1	5	4
2	1	2	5	3
3	1	3	5	2
4	2	5	10	5
5	2	7	10	3
6	3	10	15	5
7	3	13	15	2
8	4	17	20	3
9	5	22	25	3
10	6	28	30	2
11	8	36	40	4

Table Xb

Roll	Bet	Loss	Win	Net Win
1	1	1	10	9
2	1	2	10	8
3	1	3	10	7
4	1	4	10	6
5	1	5	10	5
6	2	7	20	13
7	2	9	20	11
8	2	11	20	9
9	2	13	20	7
10	2	15	20	5
11	3	18	30	12
12	3	21	30	9
13	3	24	30	6
14	3	27	30	3
15	4	31	40	9
16	4	35	40	5
17	5	40	50	10
18	5	45	50	5
19	6	51	60	9
20	7	58	70	12
21	7	65	70	5
22	8	73	80	7
23	9	82	90	8
24	10	92	100	8
25	11	103	110	7
26	12	115	120	5
27	14	129	140	11
28	15	144	150	6
29	17	161	170	9
30	19	180	190	10
31	23	203	230	27
32	24	227	240	13
33	26	253	260	7
34	30	283	300	17
35	32	315	320	5
36	36	351	360	9
37	40	391	400	9
38	45	436	450	14
39	50	486	500	14

Table Xc

Roll	Bet	Loss	Win	Net Win
1	1	1	8	7
2	1	2	8	6
3	1	3	8	5
4	1	4	8	4
5	1	5	8	3
6	2	7	16	9
7	2	9	16	7
8	2	11	16	5
9	2	13	16	3
10	3	16	24	8
11	3	19	24	5
12	3	22	24	2
13	4	26	32	6
14	4	30	32	2
15	5	35	40	5
16	6	41	48	7
17	7	48	56	8
18	8	56	64	8
19	9	65	72	7
20	10	75	80	5
21	12	87	96	9
22	13	100	104	4

Table Xd
Hardway 4 or 10

Roll	Bet	Loss	Win	Net Win
1	1	1	15	14
2	1	2	15	13
3	1	3	15	12
4	1	4	15	11
5	1	5	15	10
6	1	6	15	9
7	1	7	15	8
8	1	8	15	7
9	1	9	15	6
10	1	10	15	5
11	2	12	30	18
12	2	14	30	16
13	2	16	30	14
14	2	18	30	12
15	2	20	30	10
16	2	22	30	8
17	2	24	30	6
18	2	26	30	4
19	3	29	45	16
20	3	32	45	13
21	3	35	45	10
22	3	38	45	7
23	3	41	45	4
24	4	45	60	15
25	4	49	60	11
26	4	53	60	7
27	4	57	60	3
28	5	62	75	13
29	5	67	75	8
30	5	72	75	3
31	6	78	90	12
32	6	84	90	6
33	7	91	105	14
34	7	98	105	7
35	8	106	120	14
36	8	114	120	6

Table Xe
3 or 11

Roll No.	Bet	Loss	Win	Net Win
1	1	1	30	29
2	1	2	30	28
3	1	3	30	27
4	1	4	30	26
5	1	5	30	25
6	1	6	30	24
7	1	7	30	23
8	1	8	30	22
9	1	9	30	21
10	1	10	30	20
11	1	11	30	19
12	1	12	30	18
13	1	13	30	17
14	1	14	30	16
15	1	15	30	15
16	1	16	30	14
17	1	17	30	13
18	1	18	30	12
19	1	19	30	11
20	1	20	30	10
21	1	21	30	9
22	1	22	30	8
23	1	23	30	7
24	1	24	30	6
25	1	25	30	5
26	2	27	60	33
27	2	29	60	31
28	2	31	60	29
29	2	33	60	27
30	2	35	60	25
31	2	37	60	23
32	2	39	60	21
33	2	41	60	19

Table Xf
2 or 12

Roll No.	Bet	Loss	Win	Net Win
34	2	43	60	17
35	2	45	60	15
36	2	47	60	13
37	2	49	60	11
38	2	51	60	9
39	2	53	60	7
40	2	55	60	5
41	3	58	90	32
42	3	61	90	29
43	3	64	90	26
44	3	67	90	23
45	3	70	90	20
46	3	73	90	17
47	3	76	90	14
48	3	79	90	11
49	3	82	90	8
50	3	85	90	5
51	4	89	120	31
52	4	93	120	27
53	4	97	120	23
54	4	101	120	19
55	4	105	120	15
56	4	109	120	11
57	4	113	120	7
58	5	118	150	32
59	5	123	150	27
60	5	128	150	22
61	5	133	150	17
62	5	138	150	12
63	5	143	150	7
64	6	149	180	31
65	6	155	180	25

Roll No.	Bet	Loss	Win	Net Win
66	6	161	180	19
67	6	167	180	13
68	6	173	180	7
69	7	180	210	30
70	7	187	210	23
71	7	194	210	16
72	7	201	210	9
73	8	209	240	31
74	8	217	240	23
75	8	225	240	15
76	8	233	240	7
77	9	242	270	28
78	9	251	270	19
79	9	260	270	10
80	10	270	300	30
81	10	280	300	20
82	10	290	300	10
83	11	301	330	29
84	11	312	330	18
85	11	323	330	7
86	12	335	360	25
87	12	347	360	13
88	13	360	390	30
89	13	373	390	17
90	14	387	420	33
91	14	401	420	19
92	14	415	420	5
93	15	430	450	20
94	15	445	450	5
95	16	461	480	19

Roll No.	Bet	Loss	Win	Net Win
96	17	478	510	32
97	17	495	510	15
98	18	513	540	27
99	18	531	540	9
100	19	550	570	20
101	20	570	600	30
102	20	590	600	10
103	21	611	630	19
104	22	633	660	27
105	22	655	660	5
106	23	678	690	12
107	24	702	720	18
108	25	727	750	23
109	26	753	780	27
110	27	780	810	30
111	28	808	840	32
112	29	837	870	33
113	30	867	900	33
114	31	898	930	32
115	32	930	960	30
116	33	963	990	27
117	34	997	1020	23
118	35	1032	1050	18
119	36	1068	1080	12
120	37	1105	1110	5
121	39	1144	1170	26
122	42	1186	1260	74
123	42	1228	1260	32
124	43	1271	1290	19
125	44	1315	1320	5
126	46	1361	1380	19
127	48	1419	1440	21
128	50	1469	1500	31

Roll	Bet	Loss	Win	Net Win
1	1	1	8	7
2	1	2	8	6
3	1	3	8	5
4	1	4	8	4
5	1	5	8	3
6	2	7	16	9
7	2	9	16	7
8	2	11	16	5
9	2	13	16	3
10	3	16	24	8
11	3	19	24	5
12	3	22	24	2
13	4	26	32	6
14	4	30	32	2
15	5	35	40	5
16	6	41	48	7
17	7	48	56	8
18	8	56	64	8
19	9	65	72	7
20	10	75	80	5
21	12	87	96	9
22	13	100	104	4

Table Xg
Any Craps

Dice no	2	3	4	5	6	7	8	9	10	11	12
Field bet	2	1	1	L	L	L	L	1	1	1	2
Place bet				$\frac{7}{5}$ 1.4	$\frac{7}{6}$ 1.2	L	$\frac{7}{6}$ 1.2				

Table XI
Field/Place Combo

AN EXPERT ON YOUR FIRST TRIP

This chapter is designed to provide player exposure to the general knowledge and unique characteristics of the dice play so that when the player walks up to the crap table, no one will know but what he is an experienced gambler who lives in the casino.

First, on the ride from the plane to the casino, read the chapter, CRAP TABLE OPERATIONS. Scan it, then quickly read the chapter on the area of the table that you would like to experiment with first (i.e., Pass Line, Don't Pass, Come and etc.).

The next job is to find the gambling casino that you've selected. Enter the casino and find the crap tables. They're generally in the center of the casino. One must weave his way through all of the gambling slot machines and 21 tables.

Once you've found the crap tables, notice that there are areas for players on each side of the table. There is a dealer that manages the bets and payoffs on each side of the table. Take your paper money, toss it on the table in front of the dealer and simply say, "Change." The dealer will then convert your money into an equal quantity of chips. Don't give it to the stickman in the middle of the table; he doesn't make change.

After getting your chips, decide what area of the table that you want to bet. Keep the hands out of the table area except when betting or collecting. That's not when the shooter is throwing the dice, but between shots of the dice.

Do not drop your cigarette or cigar ashes on the table no matter how many of the house drinks you have under your belt.

When rolling the dice, shake them, spit on them, talk to them, flip them in the air, do anything you'd like but keep them away from your body and above the table. There's also a rule that you shake and do all of this with one hand so that the dice do not get battered. Do not rub them on the table. When it's your time to shoot the dice select only two dice. Throw them to the opposite end of the table. Attempt to bounce them off the opposite wall. That's what the casino likes to see. Some new players go up and grab all six or eight dice that are handed to them and throw them across the table.

The player does not have to roll or shoot the dice if he does not want to. Simply say, "Pass," "El Passo," or whatever else you would want to say so that the stickman knows that you don't want them.

There are many slang phrases that dice players use. You may want to master them, but a clear call out of the bet, exactly as you want it on the table, is sufficient. Make sure that the bet is where you want it. An improper understanding of all of this nice slang lingo could cause the bet to be put in the wrong place.

If you want free cigars, cigarettes or drinks, just tell the dealer or the table boss. He will be most pleased to see that you get them; all complimentary. If you have any questions, don't be afraid to ask the dealers. They may think you're intelligent.

When you play the Pass Line or Don't Pass, Come or Don't Come, make your own bets in that area. The dealers do not put these bets down for you. The same applies also to the Field and Big 6 and Big 8.

All proposition bets are made by tossing the chips into the center of the table to the stickman, then call out the bet which you would wish to make. For all other areas of the table, such as place bets or lays, set the proper chips on the table. Tell the table dealer what bet you would like him to make for you.

There are racks on top of the rail in which to put the chips; so put them there. Don't try stuffing them in your pockets in the middle of play. This usually results in dropping them all over the floor. Beneath the rail on the player's side are racks for drinks, ashtrays and so on. Keep your drinks there.

Standing with a drink over the table gets the boss very excited. In the event that a dice cube flys up, hits and cracks the glass, the drink would be spilled onto the table.

Some players don't hold the drink glasses too well after a few, with the same possible results.

Now you have all the basics to look like an expert on your first trip to the table. Get excited, stay cool, but look LUCKY.

DO's & DON'Ts

WHAT'S IT ALL ABOUT?

A set of basic personal rules for playing the game.

DISCUSSION

All of us try to develop some personal rules to deal with life. The dice game is just another event in life. To help the player become successful here is a list of a few of the Do's and a chance to extract the basic Don'ts of the game. No one is capable of living up to all the Do's or avoiding all the Don'ts but here's a shot at some that could work.

DO's:
1. Carefully observe all the dice action. Do this with a clear and open mind. Observe only

what is truly happening and try not to interject your desire into the game. Observe, observe, observe! Decisions should be made upon observation not on what you would like to see the game become.

2. Look for definable runs of the dice numbers. Runs are constantly occurring in a random, short-lived fashion. These runs will show up as all varieties of dice numbers, not always the Pass Line or the Don't Pass. Sometimes only Field numbers or 6's, or craps will occur repeatedly, etc., etc. Instant and accurate detection of these runs is essential. Playing the runs and being correct is the way that one has the positive advantage in this game.

3. Make investment bets only when you feel that you know what is going on in the game. Guessing is gambling. This is a game of investment; try to determine the runs. Invest when you feel you've defined a run and follow it through.

4. Once you've made the decision, go on with it. Believe a little bit in your inner inspirations and they'll grow with you. Do not allow yourself to get caught up with the external desires and hopes of all the other players. That's a constant interference in the game. All players around the table would like to see a dice game in which the Pass Line has 30 or more passes. They all know something about playing the Pass Line. These games are rare and if one wants to wait for that type of run he may grow too old and gray to play when it does occur.

5. Minimize the alcohol and heavy food

consumption. If you feel ill, don't play. Play when you're peaked out, play when your body is in good form and feels great. Particular times of the day are sometimes better for one player than another. Some players may be night owls - they do best at the thought process in the middle of the night. Other players may be morning people - early in the morning is their time. Still other players may be dinner seekers - they get a spurt of energy before dinner. Go invest and win money when it's your time thing but keep the alcohol consumption low. No one has ever seen a quick, bright, smashed gambler.

6. Once you've conceived a plan of action, carry it out precisely in every detail. Commit your decision into motion and act at once. Take no consul with the possibility of failure. Fear nothing - proceed to completion with firm materialization of the planned goal in sight. If alterations become necessary make them in the same initial conception and conviction and carry them through. One of the big downfalls of the investor is that he feels and knows a certain event will occur but he doesn't have the guts to follow up on it. Sure enough, it happens and then he says, "I knew it, I knew it," but so what? He didn't do anything about it. If you're afraid, stay away from the game. You can't win being afraid. Also, if betting with scared money, that is if you're betting a limit higher than you feel comfortable with, then you will not make good decisions. Bet the kind of bet that feels best with you.

7. Limit your time period at the craps table

to some reasonable expanse of time: 15 minutes, a half-hour or whatever is best for each individual. The craps game is a game of heavy play. It does absorb the player's energy. Hang in there for an eight hour shift and see for yourself. When the old energy bank gets low one does not do as well. Take a break, the game will be there when you get back. Play it at your best so that you can view it objectively and not through a muddled thought process.

8. Don't hesitate to insure or remove your bets if you believe you have made a bad decision. Sometimes the game looks good when you enter it and then you get the feeling that it is about over. More often than not, along with a little experience, taking advantage of these feelings will certainly pay off. Insure, remove your bet or do anything to preserve your investment capital pool.

DON'TS

All successful investors like to deal with the positive approach. The above text has provided the Do's. The Don'ts are the opposite. I'm sure that each player can withdraw his best of Don'ts from this Do process.

CRAP TABLE OPERATION

FIGURES & TABLES

Figure 1

DISCUSSION

The methods of dice table operation and payoffs vary slightly from casino to casino. Some of the smaller casinos about the world do not have crap tables at all. Usually only the larger operations will have the dice game. Some of the largest world casinos may have only eight to ten crap tables in the casino.

Before getting involved in the crap game it's advised that one find out the peculiarities about each casino, such as the minimum/maximum bet on that table, the payoffs and whether single odds, double odds or higher odds are allowed.

The dice tables are usually located somewhere in the center of the casino. The casinos are oriented toward having people walk past slot machines and other easily dispensable devices which are placed near the entrances. This will absorb the potential players small change. The crap tables are generally located in a more remote area of the casino. They know that the die-hard crap player will find them no matter where they are hidden.

Figure 1 shows a layout of the crap table operation.

The back portion of the table is generally roped off for the pit operation. Players stand on each side of the table indicated by the player arrows. There are large leaning rails around the table to help support the weary player. Racks have been constructed immediately in front of the rails for holding the players gambling chips. There are shelves below the leaning rail with room to place the cocktail glasses, ashtrays and whatever, but there are no seats to park one's dead frame.

The H2 position is the stickman. He is responsible for collecting and passing the dice to the appropriate shooter. He manages the dice, calls out the dice numbers that appear, retrieves and returns the dice to the shooter. He also manages all the bets in the proposition bet area of the table. This is located directly in front of the stickman.

The H3 and H4 dealers manage and payoff at their respective ends of the crap table. They pay off all proposition bets as directed by the stickman.

The H1 position is the table boss or boxman. Sometimes this position is filled with two people.

The table boss is responsible for the table operation. He takes the player's paper money and places it in the money slot located in front of him and issues an equivalent value of house playing chips. He also inspects the dice after each shooting player's turn or when necessary to assure that no outside dice have been entered into the game. He watches to see that the bets and payoffs are proper. He has the total accountability and financial responsibility for that particular dice table operation.

All of the table operators including the table boss are relieved about every twenty minutes to a different table position. They are relieved after forty minutes for a twenty minute break. Not bad hours, but for the H2, H3 and H4 dealers it's all heavy duty, on their feet.

The players also suffer; this standing can become a little hard on the legs, back and other areas of the body. Most of the players are not accustomed to long play periods in the vertical position.

All of the table operators have been well-schooled to be cordial, polite, tolerant and very helpful. They are generally too busy to provide much assistance on instructions of play.

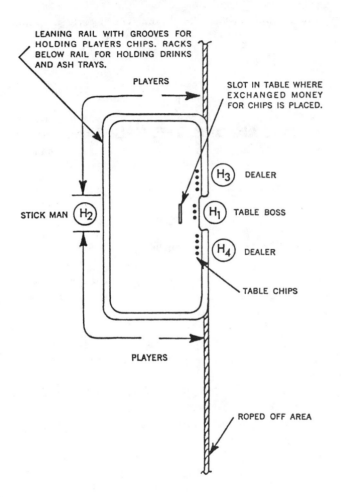

Figure 1
Crap Table Operation

AH! YES, THE CASINO

It matters not whether you visit fabulous Las Vegas, picturesque Tahoe, quaint Reno, boisterous Atlantic City, the luxurious French Riviera, Monte Carlo, the Bahamas Islands, Cairo, etc. The casinos are all lavishly decorated.

The larger gambling establishments are beautiful, ultra-modern structures that just must be visited.

They're brightly lighted with flamboyant, colorful decorations and expensive fixtures to invite the perspective gambler to a pleasant, exciting environment.

A description of the game would be incomplete unless the gambling environment had also been described and established. This environment has much impact on the player attitude for the game. The atmosphere created is exciting and friendly.

The casino employees are managed and well schooled to be cordial and helpful. The casino management personnel are among the best business men in the world. They know precisely how to manage business relative to the human psychology of released desire.

They provide an attractive environment to elevate the level of consciousness. They make sure that the potential players have the maximum of freedom, virtually free from any rules and regulations. Everything anyone would want it at his fingertips. This Disneyland for adults environment will keep the players emotionally receptive.

The entry into the casino will take you right through or very near all the gambling devices. With clatter of slot machines, clicks of the spinning roulette wheels and shouting dice players, who could resist joining the happy crowd and investing a few dollars to test their luck.

Don't expect to find spectator seats or comfortable chairs spread throughout for the viewer's relaxation. You'll find little lounging area in the casinos. This is a place of excitement and action for participating sportsmen, not spectators.

If you want to loaf, there are cocktail lounges, restaurants and other beautiful areas of entertainment for the gambling break enjoyment. The casino cannot be productive establishing spectator seats for viewers.

It is also difficult to find a clock in the casino. No one wants to remind anyone that time has any reference to the gambling system.

The water fountains are scarce and difficult to find. It's much easier to stop by the cocktail lounge or bar and procure a more tasty fluid.

If you are an active gambler, the drinks and smokes, of course, are all on the house. Free drinks will continue as long as you wish. The casino knows that alcohol will help brighten your spirits and give you that carefree, happy-go-lucky, generous feeling. Where else can you get free drinks just the way you like them and all just for the fun of it?

The casino employees maintain their courtesy and charm in this environment of rude and demanding people with little or no indication of stimuli affect. They must all be stress psychologists, saints or both.

To gamble you will have to exchange your dollars for an equal value in house chips. This marvelous technique allows the house to separate you from the money feeling. You might shudder at throwing a hard earned $5 or more upon the table and seeing it disappear, but with a $5 chip it's different somehow. It's like playing with buttons, play-money or some other type of devices that have no real money attachment.

All this marvelous atmosphere has been created just for you. It's nice to know, but one must understand that it was all created to keep one happy while they attempt their chances with the test of lady luck.

All of this allows the player to be elated if he wins, happy if he loses. After all, where can one go and be treated so fantastically? It is possible, have faith, for the astute player of the craps table to come away from the game a winner.

The major U.S. casinos, in addition to

being modern, elegant and exciting, have a large variety of interesting entertainment with a quantity of name stars that are seldom available anywhere in the world in such numbers.

The food, drinks and hospitality are delightful. It is all created and provided just for your entertainment. So visit the casino with the proper view that It's All Yours, It's All FOR FUN, and ENJOY!

A LITTLE HISTORY

WHAT'S IT ALL ABOUT?

Did gambling start in Las Vegas, or?

DISCUSSION

Probably any noted gambling state such as Nevada would not mind if the world thought that they invented gambling. Gambling history, however, goes back a long way, so far that it must be impressed genetically within our species just as our ability to digest the foods that we find desirable and consume.

Gambling goes back to time periods at least 4,000 years before Christ. Some of the first records of gambling are from the Chinese culture.

Gambling was legalized and taxed in India about 300 B.C. Egyptians used games of chance to decide the fate of criminals. Gambling flourished in Ancient Greece even though it was against the law. Greek mythology contains gambling.

Dice games were popular in Persia under King Alexander. His queen cleverly engaged the king in a game she could win by cheating to obtain his favorite slave to torture her son to death.

Emperors of Rome were avid gamblers although gambling was forbidden during their reigns. Loaded dice were discovered in the ruins of Pompeii. Romans played a form of lottery as dinner entertainment. Some of the early dice were crafted from the knuckle bones of goats and sheep.

The Old Testament contains the drawing of lot's to determine God's will. The early Christians forbid gambling but Constantinople, the seat of the church was the 13th Century gambling capitol of the world.

Leo X was a compulsive gambler. Cards appeared in England and France in the 13th Century having originated in the Far East and were carried west by tourists.

Gambling flourished in England during the reign of Richard I. Detailed rules were published on who could gamble for what.

Most all the North American Indian tribes practiced some form of gambling. Early Indian inhabitants of Clark County, Nevada, in which Las Vegas is located, used gambling instruments as far back as 2,000 years ago.

One day out of the murky past came the great state of Nevada and the development of the gambling model for the world.

Nevada accomplished statehood in 1864.

In 1869, Nevada legislators legalized gambling and established fees despite the governor's veto. Gambling continued until 1907 with various changes occurring in the law. In 1909, all gambling was prohibited. It was a felony to gamble in Nevada.

In 1915, the legislature relaxed the law allowing some gaming. In 1931, the modern era of gambling began. By 1941, gambling had increased 49% and the years between 1941 and 1944 it increased another 56%. Most gambling was in or around the Reno area. In 1940, Clark County, Nevada had only 15% of the state population; today it's the largest Nevada population center.

In December 1946, Bugsy Segal, famed gambler, opened the Flamingo Hotel. It was Nevada's first major plush resort hotel casino. Bugsy Segal had a gambling operation off the coast of California that had been shut down by the authorities.

In 1955, the legislature created a Nevada Gaming Control Board within the Nevada Tax Commission. This board established policies, eliminated undesirables and provided gaming and tax regulation.

In 1959, the Nevada Gaming Commission was created. This consisted of five members appointed by the governor. They meet once each month. The old Gaming Control Board became the enforcement arm of this commission.

In 1971, the Gaming Control Board took over all the area but gambling and denying gambling license which was left to the Tax Commission.

The Gaming Policy Committee was

established. It consists of the governor as the chairman, a member of the Gaming Commission, a member of the Gaming Control Board, two representatives from the public, and two representatives from the gaming industry.

About 50% of the Nevada workforce today have jobs because of the gaming industry. The growth in gambling in Nevada and across the country has been phenomenal.

With mass public participation in these legal gambling activities the once controversial subject of gambling has taken on a new light. Most of the remaining controversy over gambling has been left to the clergy and lawmakers while the population are thoroughly enjoying the fun of gaming.

THAT SILLY CUBE

WHAT'S IT ALL ABOUT?

Some surprising data about that little dice cube.

FIGURES & TABLES

Figure 2, Table I.

DISCUSSION

Most all of us at one time or another, in some type of game, have been associated with the dice cube; but how many times have we ever really thought about these "Silly Cubes?"

They come in all sizes. Over the years they have appeared with hearts, diamonds, numbers and letters on the surfaces. Some type of dice have appeared throughout virtually all societies in one form or another. They are considered to be among the oldest of gaming tools.

The earlier dice were a far cry from the modern, brightly colored perfect cut type of cube. The dice used in the modern gambling casinos are as nearly perfect cubes as can be constructed. They are about 3/4 of an inch on each side. They also have markings easily identifying the dice as property of a particular casino.

This allows the casino authorities, with a quick look at the dice, to determine whether the dice in play were purchased by the casino or are some others artificially introduced into the game.

Both the casino and player would prefer the perfect dice cube. This ideal dice cube would, after many rolls, more closely match the mathematically predicted distribution of dice numbers shown in Table I. This prediction is, of course, the whole basis for the payoff quantities and profit structure of the game.

Figure 2 shows an isometric drawing of the dice cube. The solid dots that appear on the surfaces are the same as that seen by the viewer. The hidden lines represent the dots on the sides not seen.

Looking at the figure, one can see in the front view that the 6 dots appear on the front. The 1 appears on the opposite or back side. The 5 is on the right side of the dice with a 2 appearing opposite the 5. The 3 is on top of the dice with a 4 appearing on the bottom.

The point to note here is that the sum of all opposite sides of the dice equals seven.

At most casinos, new dice are put into the game at the beginning of each shift. The old dice are removed and destroyed. These new dice have such perfect cut sides that the corners are extremely sharp. If they bounce off the table, in this new condition and hit someone, they can cause skin cuts and injury. By the end of the eight hours of use the corners get fairly well rounded. When one sees the combination of new dice and a wild shooter, they should consider running, ducking or bringing along the necessary safety equipment.

The ideal dice cube would be one in which the material has a homogeneous structure throughout. It would have a perfect flat cut on all surfaces and all the surfaces would be at perfect right angles to each other. Not all craps cubes are constructed in this manner.

We'll explore the change of the dice game when the materials are not as that just described or when changes have been made that affect the mass of the basic configuration and thereby the center of gravity of the cube.

Note: Most major USA casinos procure the best dice cubes that are commercially available.

TECHNICAL STUFF

Let's look at a dice cube in which holes have been drilled to indicate the dots. Paint has been placed in these holes to bring out the contrast of the dots. One can see that more material has been removed from the side having the larger quantity of dots. Less material would have been removed from the opposite side.

This would change the physics of the cube to cause the center of gravity to shift toward the side with the least material removed. This side would be heavier and would be the side to fall most often down against the table. The larger numbers would then appear more often on the up side or the dice number.

The best example of this would be with the 6 dots on one side and the one dot on the opposite side. The center of gravity would not be in the center of the cube but would be more toward the one dot side.

Any alteration of the dice affects the center of mass and the probability of the dice numbers. They would not occur like the expected mathematical distribution of Table I.

In the case where the dice are not drilled but dots are added to the sides, then one could expect that the side which has the most dots could be a slight bit heavier (if the dot material is heavier than the cube material). The center of gravity would move just the opposite of what we had previously described. It would favor the sides with the larger quantity of dots. In the above example, the 6 dots side would then have the center of gravity closer to the 6 dot side.

Sometimes the hole is filled with other types of material. The dice performance would be altered slightly. This may affect the center of gravity of the dice depending upon the specific gravity of the fill material.

One can see that in any case whether dots are added, holes are drilled , painted, filled or whatever; there is no perfect cube.

The affect on the game may be slight

depending on how much alteration has occurred.

It is noted that the opposite sides of the dice when added together equal 7. The greatest affect on the dice numbers will be increased or decreased by the largest and smallest numbered sides, such as the dice numbers 6, 1, 5 and 2. If this can be determined by an observant player, then the 2 or 12 betting system contained in the chapter, BETTING SYSTEMS, HERE'S MORE, is virtually a flawless path to riches.

The informed player should note the type of dice he's working with and change his betting techniques to take advantage of these physical properties.

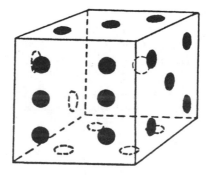

Figure 2
Crap Cube

WHO's MANAGING THE MONEY

WHAT'S IT ALL ABOUT?

Does anybody know where all their money is going?

FIGURES & TABLES

Figure 12

DISCUSSION

Unless you've brought your accountant along or have a computerized system that will give you an instantaneous status of your capital investment/venture, then one needs help. The best aid would be a simple money management system. One that will allow the player to know his status at all times during the play.

The species of man has a desire to procure which is generally much greater than his ability to produce. When it comes to gambling it gets even worse. When one starts to lose, it's natural to want to bet (a lot) more trying to play catch-up. As one begins to win it is also natural to back off, thereby limiting the quantity one could win. It turns out that in gambling this natural desire is the wrong approach.

There are probably an infinite variety of ways to mishandle money - at least as many ways as there are individual creators of ways to do it. So in case you don't already have a specific way to manage the money, here is a group of suggested examples of the way it might be done.

In Figure 12, one can see that the chips have been arranged in a nice, neat order. They also have been arranged so that at a glance the player can determine the quantity of chips that he has available (in the rail). One can know status by the relative position of chips on hand versus what he had when he entered the game. Keeping a simple system like this takes little effort and at a glance the player can determine his status.

Keeping some system like this is far better than continually attempting to count the chips while missing out on all the action at the table.

The player is at the table to make his fortune, isn't he? He, therefore, shouldn't be distracted by trying to keep track of everything else. Keep it simple - spread it out so that it can easily be seen. Organize it into simple categories which require virtually no effort on the player's part.

Figure 12 is only a suggested arrangement. The player can expand upon this. Some players stack the chips vertically and parallel on the table in groups of hundreds, twenty-fives or whatever denomination is convenient. They may use different color chips inbetween to signify hundreds, thousands or whatever markers one would like to know about.

Managing the money is at the least a nuisance overhead. You're there to play and not worry about the money. It's important that it be kept as carefree an item as possible.

Other than status, another necessary area of money management is to have available the proper quantities and varieties of betting chips. This will allow one to have the change to make the right kind of bets as one would like.

It would be embarrassing to miss out on the return of all that investment capital simply because one couldn't get the chips bet on the proper area at the right time. As the player converts his paper money to chips he needs to keep this in mind so that he can tell the table dealer what quantity of each type of chip he wants.

If for some reason the disorganization has occurred and you don't have the proper betting chips, by all means call the bet out to the table dealer. He will usually accept that bet and allow you to pay him later. At least the bet is in process according to your wish.

Another important part of money management is how much of a loss/limit pool does one set?

Does one go into the game with $100, $300, $500, $1000 or ?. This depends upon the size of the unit bet which the player feels comfortable in making. If you're a $5 bettor then you don't need as big a pool as you would if you were a $100 per bet player.

We are all familiar with the old addage, "It takes money to make money." I would like to interject: "It takes money to lose money." Certainly a person with $100 cannot lose $1,000 and one with $1,000 cannot lose $100,000. With gambling, one can only lose what he has brought with him to gamble plus his credit limit at the casino. No one is going to lose his house because he can't bet it on the table. One can, however, borrow money against the house and take the money to the casino as funds to gamble.

It's far more important in the gambling money management system for the individual to have his money working at all times rather than attempting to make a lot of money work only a few times. The player needs to develop what is known as a loss/limit pool of money. It he's a $1 bettor, something in the neighborhood of $30 to $100 may be adequate; for a $5 bettor, $100 to $300; for a $10 bettor, $300 to $1,000 and for a $20 bettor, $1,000 to $3,000.

The selected amount is strictly up to the individual but the fund must be of sufficient size to allow continuous small losses and still have a reserve of capital to take advantage of runs, when they occur. There is no absolute answer to the loss/limit question. Each player should develop his own comfortable position. What it listed above is a suggested range. It may not be adequate for a particular gambler.

The worst thing that could happen to a gambler is to establish too small a loss/limit and be at a game where he has just expended the last of his funds. On the very next roll the game turns. If he would have been in it he would have made a fortune.

He now has developed a psychological hook. On his next trip, he will probably bring too large a loss/limit pool believing that if he has enough money he will see it to a turn around game. He's now a dreaming gambler, no longer a playing investor. If one hits the complete expenditure of his loss/limit pool, stop - take a break - the craps game will still be there some other day. One will also be in a better position to deal with the game.

When it comes to expending and returning money from and to the rail (your loss/limit pool), common sense should prevail. Generally, the ideal way one should spend money from the pool is to make only token bets. As wins begin to occur, return some money to the pool and increase the bets. In this manner one can preserve the pool size and always be betting with profit capital. This is like a small business man who takes $1,000 and opens a business. He doesn't try to buy the building next door until he has increased his profit enough to be able to afford it.

Dealing with failure is easy. If a player goes to the table and begins to lose until he has reached the limit of all the gambling funds his solution is very simple and very definite. When he's out of money; he's out of gambling. The most difficult problem one faces is dealing with success. What about a player who goes to the craps table, invests and finds that his pool is growing dramatically. Soon he is filthy rich. How does he decide what to do? Does he continue until he owns the casino or does he decide to take his profit and leave? Deciding when to quit while a winner is the major problem of all gamblers. This area will be explored more in the chapter, HOW TO WIN.

Managing money is like planning and managing one's life. If you don't do it, someone else surely will.

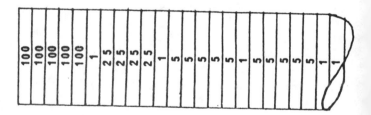

Figure 12
Chip Accounting

THE CRYSTAL BALL

WHAT'S IT ALL ABOUT?

Taking advantage of moments of intuitive perception, if one ever gets them!

DISCUSSION

Probably everyone at some time in their life has had moments of inspiration or perception when they feel that they know exactly how a specific event is going to occur.

During the times that these strong feelings exist, the accuracy of prediction is very high. Rarely, however, does anyone react to the validity of this perception. Most of the people having these moments of heightened intuitivity express immediately after the event, "I knew it was going to happen like that." They generally do nothing about the event before it happens.

Some players may be able (at times) to throw dice and have whatever number they want simply appear. These occurrences defy the probability of it being pure chance. There's no scientific explanation for all of this to date. Certainly gazing into the crystal ball for prediction is not an acceptable answer.

Experimentation in the area of this phenomena has been conducted in many laboratories and various universities around the world. The main problem with research on the subject is repeatability. It just comes and goes. It's generally not something that one can sit down and will into existence. It seems to just happen.

The intent in this discussion is for information; not to infer that each and every one can perceive a major set of events or runs on a table and take advantage of them on every trip to the casino.

This information is only presented here to bring attention to the phenomena. The perspective player, if aware of this phenomena, may act. Should it occur, he can perhaps recognize it and take advantage of it to prosper from such good fortune.

Observations indicate that this perception occurs more frequently under great emotional stress or need. Mentally unstable persons at times have periods of pure perception. So if you get a little crazy at the crap table perhaps that's the catalyst necessary to produce this phenomena for you.

Some may call this phenomena luck or say that they're having a great day. It matters little by what name you call it. If you're lucky enough to have it happen to you, if you're observant enough to detect it, if you take advantage of it and if it works for you, then by all means, <u>use it</u>!

INVEST, DON'T GAMBLE

WHAT'S IT ALL ABOUT?

What is the difference between an investor and a gambler?

DISCUSSION

Generally when we think of an investor, we think of a person who saves up a pile of money to invest. He then seeks out, through some long process, a type of an investment that interests him, usually one that he feels will provide a growth of his investment funds.

Unless the investor has been led astray by some scheming, unscrupulous person, he usually does, over a long period of time, get some realistic growth. The hard-earned capital which he put into the investment becomes larger, at least in dollar size.

What is a gambler? Well, you probably

know, you've no doubt heard reports from your friends, neighbors and other perspective gambling city visitors.

You may have heard statements like, "I have taken $300 ($1000 or whatever) to gamble and when that's gone, that's it." Is this a common statement that you've heard many times?

Let's examine this statement in some finer detail. The first thing I'd like to examine is, "Does anyone believe them?" If they've taken $300 to gamble, then I believe they probably also have either a line of credit or have more stashed away in the event that they would still like to gamble a little more. Secondly, the statement, "When it's gone" indicates that the player expects to lose. Expects to lose. This statement contains expectations of losses, not wins.

On the contrary, an investor might say, "I've taken $1000 and put it into this investment. When it brings me a gain of 50% then I shall withdraw the gained funds and buy a new stove with it." The investor expects to get back his invested capital plus a profit. Expects to win!

Why does the gambler insist on betting it all? Does this not lead to the idea that even if he won double, triple, or ?, he's going to go for all or broke. All or broke. What is this greed of ALL? Where does it stop? This indicates that if he'd taken his $300 and had won $10,000 with it, that the gambler would have said, "Ah, I've won $10,000. Now I will gamble this $10,000. I'll own the casino or I'll have nothing. I'll own the city or I'll have nothing, and etc." The gambler has no clear focus on what size win is large enough to fulfill his ALL lust. If he did stop with the $10,000 win, he will always wonder, could he have made more if he had stayed in the game?

We all know when he'll stop. The casino knows and depends upon this human trait for its grand profits. He will stop gambling when he has lost it all. The profit, the gambling funds and whatever he can get his hands on easily.

The gambling attitude is probably becoming apparent to all by now. How does a gambler become an investor? The truth is that not many do and that's the biggest reason that most everyone loses at gambling. In fact, the casino would shudder at the thought of having this pointed out to the players if they believed that any significant number of players would change. It would devastate their profitable business.

If one who reads this book can look at this as an investment in the game of craps, then he would say to himself, "I'm going with a bankroll of $1000 and when I win 50%, $500, then I have made a successful investment. I have accomplished my goal. I will quit and take the money and enjoy my stay in Las Vegas."

The above paragraph is just an example to emphasize the investment approach. See the chapter, WHO'S MANAGING THE MONEY, for suggested pool sizes and loss limits.

The few that can understand this point, and it may appear to be a fine point, but investing versus gambling is the key that will change one's thought process into making a gain on their investment. If one can accomplish this then they have made a giant step with a new approach into the world of gaming.

Certainly not with all games can one have a complete view of the action and be able to do something about. For example: slot machines; there's little or no control that a player has over these machines as far as being able to make a decision that would affect the outcome. He puts in the money, pulls the handle and what comes up, comes up.

On the craps table the player has a view of the action. He can gain insight into the game. He can bet based upon some predetermined judgement. He has most all of the factors available to him; right in front of him. These are not generally available to an investor on most speculative investments.

Let's compare, for instance, the investment on the craps table versus an investment in the stock market. The investor, investing on the stock market may look at the charts. He may call his broker and get data on a particular stock. All of it is old data; history, yesterday's news. He makes the best choice that he can based upon whatever factors he has decided to plug into his investment formula and makes his investment. He has absolutely no knowledge or control over the system. He has no data on what is currently going on within the company. He doesn't even know the factors that create the business within the company. Also foreign to him is the specific day by day ventures, mergers, movements that are going to cause the rapid growth or rapid decay of this company's stock position.

At the craps table he has full view of what's going on. He knows the exact odds of the game. He does, if he has read and understands this book. He can see the action - what's happening right in front of him. He can make his decision based upon the real live action at the moment. He does not have to depend upon someone's recommendation through four tiers of management on what stock needs to be dumped and how to dump it, etc., etc.

The crap table is a far better investment vehicle than the stock market in this author's opinion. This is not true for all investments but for the individual investor attempting to play the stock market, it certainly is.

After reading this chapter if any of this makes sense to the individual player, he may want to consider making the winning move from the gambler's corner to the investor's side of the CRAP game.

WINNER / LOSER, WHAT'S NEXT

WHAT'S IT ALL ABOUT?

The big question mark; what are your motivations for going to a gambling city?

DISCUSSION

Many people that go to a city of gambling seem to run from one casino to the next, gambling like crazy. They do this as if that was the only reason for their visit. Maybe it is!

Most hustle from one device to the next, stay up all night, drink and smoke too much, eat excessively and do all of the things that are detrimental to good performance and health. When it's all over one may wonder what the fun was all about. It seems that with some the visit ends with blurry-eyed, punchy and broke. They might wonder, "Did I have fun?"

If this was the entire purpose of the trip, then any observer would be able to inform the visitor that they have accomplished the intended task very well.

For those that may have intended to do a variety of fun things, the same observer would tell them that they have failed.

What are the objectives of an individual's trip? Obviously, if the objectives are to see how many machines, different devices one can play in a variety of casinos in the shortest period of time, then it's a matter of getting there, collecting all the funds and going after it.

If the individual is looking for some type of balanced entertainment then they need to make the point of doing so. Quite often this is not what happens with most visitors going to a gambling city. They plan, at least initially, to do all kinds of fun things in addition to some gambling. When they get to the resort, they get caught up in the whirlwind of gambling and do little else. When they're broke they find that they have plenty of time to do other things. The funds may be too low by then to do so.

They may plan on going to the shows, eating some of the fabulous food, seeing some of the other great entertainment, catching some pool time, some sun and enjoying the recreational facilities.

The approach I'm about to present may appear a little corny and be too practical. However, try this for what one might enjoy on a vacation to a gambling resort city.

Sit down before leaving home, write up

the objectives, even specify how many hours will be spent gambling. Plan the type of shows to see, other entertainment, recreational facilities to visit, where to eat, what fine foods to sample and so on.

Upon arriving at the city, implement the schedule, try to stick by the agenda. Now, if one is fortunate enough to be a big winner in the process; then he will have money to enjoy all of what they might have considered doing and more, by utilizing this additional gambling win money. If they lose, then at least they had a great well rounded trip doing exactly what they had planned to do. They would have enjoyed these marvelous resorts that were established just for vacationing people looking for a great time.

Too often one may overhear (the couple scene) on a plane leaving Las Vegas. The woman saying, "Oh, yes, we were planning on doing this and doing that and doing the other, but hubby lost all the money the first thing and then we couldn't afford it," or "He didn't do as well as he expected," or "I lost more than I had expected and we didn't do,".....we didn't do...... We didn't do seems to be the big by-words of these marvelous gambling cities. Yet these cities have every conceivable exciting entertainment available for the benefit of the visitors.

The intended message in this chapter is that whether you win or lose, you should enjoy yourself. Set some of the money aside to enjoy yourself <u>first</u> no matter what the gambling turns out to be. If you win, don't run back to try to take the casino. Enjoy some of the winnings.

Do something good for yourself. Give yourself a real extra-special vacation with it. One might set aside a portion of the winnings to go back and gamble if desired but don't throw it all back into the casino's pocket. Don't miss out on all the fun provided by the exciting gambling resort cities.

WHAT ABOUT PROBABILITY

WHAT'S IT ALL ABOUT?

It is a description of the mathematics associated with the crap table probability.

DISCUSSION

This text was prepared for that individual who is interested in the mathematical basis for the probability prediction of the dice game. It is not designed for those just interested in playing the game nor those needing to know how to play the game. The rest of the text contains all of the data necessary to do that.

Probability is a mathematical basis for predicting the outcome of an event. It is the ratio of the outcomes that would produce a given event to the total number of possible outcomes. For the dice game we will express this in a simple mathematical formula of:

$$P = \frac{m}{n}$$

Where: P is the probability of the event happening.

n is the total number of ways in which the event can occur.

m is the way in which any single event could occur.

Looking specifically at the dice cube, Figure 2, there are six sides to each cube. Each side has dots representing the numerical value of that surface.

There are two dice cubes used for each roll. For any one surface of one cube that could be positioned surface up, there is one of the six surfaces on the other cube that could also appear up. This is true for both of the dice cube arrangements. This makes a total available surface arrangements that could appear on any roll of the dice to be thirty-six. n would then equal thirty-six. The m in the formula is the numbers of ways to make a specific dice number (2 thru 12) as it would appear taking two surfaces at a time.

Let's look at an example of calculating the probability for dice number 2. This can only be made with 1 dot appearing on one cube and 1 dot appearing on the other cube. There is, therefore, only one way to make the dice number 2. In our formula m would equal one. n will always be the same fixed value which equals thirty-six. Probability of a dice number two appearing would be one in thirty-six or one to thirty-six.

In the general gambling circles the probability of an event happening is not used. What is used is the probability of its failure to happen. These are inverse expressions of each other. It is expressed where the larger number always precedes the smaller such as 2 to 1, 3 to 2 and etc. This formula is:

$$q = \frac{n}{m}$$

Where: q is the probability of an event failing to happen. Table I and the general text uses the most common expressed probability q.

Table I has conveniently listed all of these probabilities for the player so that it's not necessary for him to even understand probability to determine what his chances are for obtaining a particular dice number.

In Table I, probability is referred to as Odds since that is the common sport terminology for probability. In the second column of Table I these Odds or probability are expressed for each dice number.

For the individual who would like to calculate the probability for each of these dice numbers, Table I will make a helpful answer quide.

WHO GAMBLES, WHY, WHO CARES

Have you ever wondered how many people gamble? Who are they? What makes one want to gamble? If you have, then you are probably like the majority of your friends, neighbors, and etc., who also have the same questions.

There has been virtually no research done on this subject. What portion of the population gambles? What are the social, religious and economic factors involved? What are the preference of gambling devices of each professional or economic level and etc.?

The few surveys that have been performed on gambling are highly subjective and represent a poor basis of knowledge.

Probably one of the reasons that it is so difficult to get information on gambling is that, the general public is very reluctant to discuss gambling even though they might personally gamble in several areas. Some of those areas may be with friends on cards, Bingo, baseball/football pools and even trips to cities that have casino gambling.

People just rarely want to discuss with anyone else whether they do gamble and how much. It appears that this is a highly personal area of activity with most people. Who gambles? Nearly everyone.

In attempting to address the question of why one gambles, from observation of friends, acquaintances, and associates in various social/economic levels, some suggestive conclusions have been drawn:

a) It seems that most, if not all, do enjoy the game of chance at some level.

b) The people on the very low economic level may gamble with numbers or on sports pools, lottery, paycheck poker, local card games, something of that nature. They lack the financial income and the mobility for large wagers.

c) The middle and upper classes may be more prone to take vacations. These vacations would lead, of course, to cities that would have casinos and casino type gambling.

In summary, it appears that almost all of us do like to gamble, no matter what the religious, social, or economic background of the individual. Some people with certain strict professed religious beliefs may think that the type of chance-taking they are making in cards with friends or other games is not gambling. In fact, the whole public seems to address gambling at the level in which they participate as being purely normal, not really gambling, a nobody's business type of activity.

Certainly the attitude is that it is not the business of law enforcement to control their gambling activities. It is all right for law enforcement to handle the syndicate gambling, mugs and thugs but on their level of gambling, it's purely okay.

In attempting to address the question of why we gamble; we will find a whole open field of theories. I am sure that anyone's theory (or excuse) is as reasonable as anyone else's. The following suggests a whole group of theories that might apply and stir the imagination of those interested in this subject:

a) Since we are a nation of movie hero makers and hero worshippers, perhaps our urges come from this manifestation of idealism. Our heros take risks, play to win against all odds, gamble their very lives. In fact, we tend to look down upon people who always play it safe.

b) Perhaps it's a normal reaction. A relief from our normal hum-drum lives.

c) Maybe it is genetic; a reflection of self-preservation.

d) A need to beat the system; beating the game of life.

e) A vehicle for expression.

f) Controlling our fate.

g) Venting our frustrations.

h) Achieving recognition.

i) A harmless indulgence in fantasies of windfall profits; buying hope.

j) A need for an opportunity to make decisions in an ever increasingly regulated world.

k) Maybe it facilitates and fulfills a

personal need for sociability and informal social interaction.

l)   Escape from a tedious and purposeless occupation.

m)   Perhaps an interest in creating equitable distribution for payment of worth.

n)   Relief from insurmountable economical and social obstacles.

o)   Relief from stress on personal initiative.

p)   Escape from loneliness.

q)   A leveler of all class distinction.

r)   A need for courageous display.

The above contains a long list of possible reasons why. I am sure that many reading this text could also come up with a few specific additional theories.

Why do we gamble? Who knows. Each individual will have to decide that for himself, if it's important at all.

Who cares about who gambles? Probably nobody, since everybody, well nearly everybody seems to like gambling in one form or another. It's probably nobody's business, anyway.

In nearly all of the states of the United States, legalized gambling is allowed in one form or another. It may appear as horse-racing, dog-racing, lottery, Jai-Alai, card clubs, Bingo or in some other form. It is very commonplace in the normal employee work groups for people to establish their own gambling games. These may be created as checkpools, baseball games, football games, or individual bets with personal friends on the outcome of various sporting events. The local guys/gals may get together for various card games including an exchange of monetary value of one form or another. All of this indicates a strong human desire to wager.

Could one become addicted to gambling? Perhaps, there are some that may. If one had a friend who became an alcoholic, he would no doubt have apathy for the addiction. However, he wouldn't suggest a ban on alcohol for the rest of the population that may enjoy the moderate usage of it. There are few that would consider banning gambling because of the very, very few who might become addicted to the activity.

With casino type of gambling, it is virtually impossible for the individual who may be addicted to gambling, to get into too much trouble through impulsive wagers. The casino clears a sufficient amount of gambling credit for an individual who desires credit. That's his limit in gambling at the casino. He can't put his car, boat, airplane, house, or anything else on the table as a wager. If one is addicted to gambling, he will have to become very innovative, on his own, to get into much of a financial bind.

GOING FOREIGN

If one wishes to be a world gambler, it would be far better if he first visited the foreign casinos and then came back to the great United States of America. To do the reverse is kind of like going uphill backwards. Foreign casinos just don't have a fraction of the sparkle created by our homeland establishments.

There's no place in the world like the fabulous Las Vegas, Nevada. All other U.S. gambling cities take some order of preference behind that.

In foreign countries such as The Bahamas, The French Riviera, Monte Carlo, Cairo, London and etc., the gambling action, especially the craps game is sparse. When one does find a crap table in action, however, it is operated essentially the same way. The table layout is almost identical to the U.S. tables and the payoffs may vary slightly but basically are the same.

In the Bahamas Islands, especially on

Grand Bahamas Island the dice tables are square and not the conventional oval shaped tables. The payoff is a little better in one or two areas of the table. Other than that the games are operated about the same.

In the areas of foreign gambling there just doesn't seem to be as many people interested in the crap table as one would see in the U.S. In Cairo, for example, the two most popular hotels that have casinos do have a crap table. The crap table operates only during the heightened vacation seasons when there are hordes of gamblers available to test their luck. The rest of the time the crap table just occupies casino space. There is no crew on hand to operate the table due to low player interest.

Most foreign casinos do not depend upon the general population for their gambling revenue. It is the upper class or visiting businessmen who they depend upon to fill their establishments. Some countries have laws prohibiting the local population from gambling.

The foreign businessmen who operate casinos certainly do not have the glamorous know-how of the fabulous Las Vegas casino managers. They do not create as free or comfortable environment as do the U.S. businesses. There is not an easy feeling with all of the freebies available. They all appear less warm and more stuffy and sophisticated with little participating gambling feeling.

There is nothing that can compare to the casinos in the United States. Although some, especially the French Riviera, have beautiful architectural structures.

I graciously challenge each of you to find this out for yourself.

Big Red - Proposition Bet Area Seven "7".

Boxcars - Dice Number 12.

C - Craps Dice Numbers 2, 3 & 12 .

Casino - The area of the hotel or building that contains the gambling devices.

Cold Table - A table where the runs of dice numbers are favorable to the Don't Pass and Don't Come player.

Comeout Roll - The first roll of a new shooter or any roll of an existing shooter for those playing the come or don't come or another specific area of the table.

C & E - Craps & eleven, dice numbers 2, 3, 12 & 11.

Craps - Dice Numbers 2, 3 and 12.

Dealers - Dice Table Operators that maintain proper betting and payoff.

Dice Runs - Rolls of the dice where some pattern of numbers continue to appear more frequently and others less frequently than the expected mathematical random distribution.

Do Bettor - Player who favors betting the pass line and come areas of the table.

Don't Bettor - Player who favors betting the don't pass and don't come areas of the table.

E - Eleven, Dice number 11

E.O. - This is an expression used by gamblers for dice number 11.

Hot Table - A table where the runs of dice numbers are favorable to the pass line and come players.

House - The owner, operator, or establishment responsible for the gambling devices.

Nena - Dice number 9.

Odds - A ratio of the likelihood of one thing occurring rather than another. A ratio expressing the probability of an event or outcome.

Off - No action on a particular bet.

Off & Down -No action on a particular bet and the return of those bet chips to the player.

On - Return to action for a particular bet which has been "off".

Pairs - Dice rolls where both dice have the same number exposed.

Pair of Ducks - Hardway 4.

Pass - To reject one's turn to roll the dice.

Pit Boss - The manager and supervisor of all the dice tables contained in a particular area of the casino.

Player - A gambler making bets upon the dice table.

Press - An expression used when a player wants his original bet doubled. The dealer just returns the payoff amount greater than that which it takes to double his bet.

Probability - Synonomous with odds.

Runs - See dice runs.

Roll - A Pass Line hand. A streak of luck.

Seven Out - Rolling a 7 after the shooter has obtained a passline point.

Shills - Casino employees that stand around and play the gambling devices to make the casino appear busy and attractive to perspective gamblers.

Shooter - A player who is actually throwing the
two dice cubes.

Snake Eyes - Dice number 2.

Stick Man - The dice table dealer that collects
the thrown dice and returns them to the
shooter. He also acts as the
controller over the proposition bet
area of the table.

Table Boss - The dice table operators sitting
between the house dealers. He has the
supervisory and financial obligation
for that dice table. Sometimes
referred to as Boxman.

The Point - Dice numbers 4, 5, 6, 8, 9 or 10
which appear on the Comeout roll
for the Pass Line players.

Working - Synonomous with "on".

NOTES: 1. All percentages are rounded off to
the nearest whole number, i.e., 2.8%
would be expressed as 3%.

2. All percentages, unless otherwise
specified, are calculated based upon
any one roll of the dice. They are
not expressed as an expected outcome
over the long range statistical
prediction.